© Cultural China Series

Jin Zhilin

CHINESE FOLK ARTS

Multiple Forms and Cultural Implications

Translated by Jin Bei

CHINA
INTERCONTINENTAL
PRESS

图书在版编目（CIP）数据

中国民间美术：英文／靳之林著；金蓓译．—2版．—北京：
五洲传播出版社，2010.1

ISBN 978-7-5085-1691-2

I.①中… Ⅱ.①靳…②金… Ⅲ.①民间工艺－工艺美术－简介－中国
－英文 Ⅳ.①J528

中国版本图书馆 CIP 数据核字（2009）第 191267 号

CHINESE FOLK ARTS
Multiple Forms and Cultural Implications

Author: Jin Zhilin

Translator: Jin Bei

Executive Editor: Deng Jinhui

Art Director: Yang Jingfei

Photo Credit: Jin Zhilin

Publisher: China Intercontinental Press (6 Beixiaomachang, Lianhuachi Donglu, Haidian District, Beijing 100038, China)

Tel: 86-10-58891281

Website: www.cicc.org.cn

Printer: C&C Joint Printing Co., (Beijing) Ltd.

Format: 720 × 965mm   1/16

Edition: Jan. 2010, 2nd edition, 3rd print run

Price: RMB 92.00 (*yuan*)

Contents

Introduction

In the early 1970s, I left the College of Fine Arts where I had been a teacher for many years and went to live in Yan'an, Shaanxi, on the Loess Plateau on the middle-upper reaches of the Yellow River. This was the home base for my research on Chinese folk art. Rich with glorious historical culture, this place had kept its long-standing cultural tradition due to generations of self-enclosed culture and years of underdeveloped transportation. As a result, the native Chinese culture was by and well maintained. In my 13 years working in the Yan'an Mass Art Museum and the Commission of Antiques Management, I had the chance to conduct on-site research in folk art, fork custom and culture, and an overall study and exploration of archaeological culture. The first-hand study of folk culture and customs, as well as its intersection with archaeological culture and historical/legendary documents, helped me get in-depth in the study of Chinese cultural and philosophical origins. From there, I went on to the Yangtze River valley, the Liaohe River basin, and the Pearl River valley, then covered the entire country from Xinjiang to Shandong to Taiwan, from Heilongjiang to Hainan Island. Since the 1990s, I traveled further, to India, Pakistan, West Asia, Turkey, Egypt and Greece, Italy, and other parts of the European and American continent, continuing my research on folk culture and archaeological and historical cultures. Putting Chinese folk culture and its cultural and philosophical origin against the larger cultural background of all mankind, I shifted my study to mankind's common cultural consciousness, and the original features of individual national cultures and philosophies.

When I reached the villages on the Loess Plateau, I found

The author at the site of Chinese New Year's fair in rural Shaanxi.

Chinese folk arts in the forms of paper-cutting, embroidery and floury flower everywhere. Some were representations of animals, such as the turtle, the snake, the fish and the frog; and some were half-human, half-animal: a human face on a turtle's body, or on the body of a snake, frog or fish. There were also wholly humanized fairies. These art works embraced the development and transformation of totem culture through three phases from matriarchal society to patriarchal society. I felt as if I were in a world of totem culture, visiting the cultural center of a tribe of ancient times. The design of a pair of fish with human faces found on painted pottery and the "fish net" code from the 6,000-year-old Yangshao Culture unearthed in Banpo of Xi'an, Shaanxi, are still quite popular in the rural area here. The designs remain among the people as symbols of the god of life and propagation, a symbol of with supernatural power.

Likewise, the color painting "Dancing dolls," with five babies

Yangshao Culture

Yangshao Culture is a Neolithic culture 5,000 to 7,000 years ago. It was first discovered in Yangshao Village of Mianchi County, Henan Province, in 1921. Yangshao Culture is mainly distributed in the midstream and downstream of Yellow River with western part of Henan Province, basin of Weihe River in Shaanxi Province and strake in the southwestern part of Shanxi Province as its center and reaching the middle of Hebei Province on the east, midstream and upstream of Han River on the south, basin of Taohe River in Gansu Province on the west, and Hetao area of Inner Mongolia on the north. Hundreds of cultural remains have been exhumated and the cultural relic unearthed reflects the same cultural characteristics. Plus, Yangshao culture period is the most glorious period of the painted pottery during the Neolithic Age in China.

Majiayao Culture

Majiayao Culture is the culture of the late Neolithic Age existing in the upper reaches of Yellow River. It is named after the site discovered in Majiayao Village, Lintao, Gansu Province, in 1923. Majiayao Culture existed around 5,000–4,000 years ago. Majiayao people made a large quantity of refined pottery in their daily life, of which painted pottery was especially excellent. Of the burial pottery unearthed in Majiayao Site, 80% is painted pottery.

hand-in-hand on painted pottery from the 5,000-year-old Majiayao Culture unearthed in Qinghai Province is also a popular paper-cut in today's folk art and customs. The five dolls (representing fairies from five directions—east, west, north, south and the center) are regarded as patron saints of the baby with coiled hair, who drives away evil spirits. The excavated antiques couldn't speak, but the old grandmother still living in the caves on the Loess Plateau gave a detailed explanation: in today's customs, people still follow the same cultural codes from 5,000–6,000 years ago.

After the Yellow River basin, I went on to the Yangtze River valley. When my journey reached the countryside of Pingxiang, Jiangxi, between the Dongting Lake and Poyang Lake, mid-stream in the Yangtze River, the culture of exorcism was ubiquitous and overwhelming. There was a Nuo God (old temple for exorcism) every five *li* (2.5 kilometers); and a General (god for exorcism) every 10 *li* (5 kilometers). Face masks, rituals, dance and theatrical play were related to exorcism and dispelling evil, as well as to a humanized all-powerful god wearing ox horns who opened up the mountain at the beginning of the world. Once again, I felt lost in a world of totem culture going back into the ancient times.

According to historical record, this area used to be the center of the Miao-Li tribal group headed by Chiyou, a legendary figure. Members of the tribal group were known to wear bronze ox horn totem masks to appear as ox heads in human bodies. This was confirmed by the excavation of ox-horn bronze masks and the mould in the area. Later, when I was in Miao villages in the mountain area of Guizhou Province, upstream in the Yangtze River, I found the same culture of exorcism. The Miao people who worshiped the ox totem believed that Chiyou, the humanized god wearing ox-head on a human body, was their ancestor. His home was originally in the Hunan and Jiangxi area. In the wake of a defeat against the Yan-Huang tribal group, the Miao tribe migrated through a number of different regions to arrive in Guizhou. The fact that there was no temple for exorcism in Guizhou, nor unearthed bronze ox-horn masks and porcelain bases, proves this historical legend.

Existing customs, take Chinese folk arts as an example, could be regarded as the living fossil of Chinese primitive culture. Archaeologists conduct their studies based on excavated antiques and cultural relics; historians refer to written records and historical documents. However, antiques are silent and opinions on historical records and legends vary. It is often hard to differentiate falsity from truth. In the event that no antiques are unearthed or no historical are available, the study becomes suspended. As one of the four most ancient civilizations, China has followed a long, uninterrupted course of culture and tradition. With its multi-ethnic population, vast territory and other unique historical and geographical conditions, China's cultural relics, even those from ancient times, are still preserved in today's folk art, customs and culture. This is especially true in the areas where major tribes of primitive society lived and tribal culture first began. These tribes are the ancestors of ancient Chinese civilization. At the peak of

The author at the site of "Yu Zhu Long" (Jade Dragon with a Pig Head) excavated from the Liaohe River basin.

Hongshan Culture "Yu Zhu Long" (Jade Dragon with a Pig Head) from the primitive society.

tribal culture, both natural disasters and man-made catastrophes had dealt major damage to the ecology of the region. The area then became culturally enclosed with limited transportation to and from outside world. As a result, Chinese culture and philosophy in their original tribal forms, represented in folk art, can still be found in today's society and cultural life. Buried antiques cannot speak, but the living antiques speak for themselves.

As the fountain spring of the ideologies of a hundred schools of thought during the period of the Spring and Autumn and Warring States periods (770–221 BC), the original Chinese philosophical system continues to be the ideological base and core content of today's folk art. It remains intact, embedded in a variety of art works, and pervades all aspects of people's social life.

The creators of Chinese folk art come from the working class masses of China's rural areas. They are mostly female laborers. A communal art, folk art would engender all of Chinese literature and all later art. Its presence is evident in everyday food, clothing, shelter and transportation; in traditional festivals, ceremonies and rituals; and in beliefs and taboos. As a living example of cultural heritage, it shows the continuity of Chinese culture from primitive society to present, a culture that bears distinct national and geographical characteristics. With this heritage, Chinese culture boasts the longest history and the richest historical sources, and of all cultures, considers itself the most widely shared and the most geographically distinct. Its cultural implication and art form accumulate a historical culture of over 7,000–8,000 years dating back to primitive society today. Its values extend far beyond the art itself;

it embodies values deeply rooted in philosophy, aesthetics, art, archaeology, history, and the study of the social sciences, the humanities, and nations. Chinese folk art also exhibits the entire nation's philosophical viewpoint, cultural ideology, emotional and psychological makings.

Life and propagation are the basic instincts of all living things in the universe. Human consciousness of life and propagation is at the heart of the ideology of *yin-yang*. Simplified, *yin-yang* revolves around the belief that the composition of *yin-yang* creates life, which, through propagation, never ends. This is the view of the universe in original Chinese philosophy, first developed in primitive society 6,000–7,000 years ago. Like the passing of human heritage by biological genes, the passing of national culture from one age to another also depends on cultural genes preserved from a nation's cultural and philosophical origin. Chinese folk art is an example of such cultural inheritance. This book will thus introduce and interpret folk art from that perspective.

Six Characteristics of Chinese Folk Art

Chinese folk art is a visual art created by ordinary people to meet ordinary social needs.

The definition of folk art is relative to the definition of the art of imperial palace, the art of aristocrats, and the art of scholars and of the literati, or professional artists. Firstly, it is a communal art created by millions in the working class, not the work of a few career artists. It is the art of the laborers, not the professionals; it is amateur, not specialized. Secondly, its social function makes it an art of necessity, used in everyday life, production, rites and ceremonies, and beliefs and taboos. It was not intended as a commercial commodity, nor to serve political needs.

Looking back on history to the age of primitive society, communal art was created by the Chinese people alongside the creation of tools, shelter and other basic appliances necessary in daily life. The emergence of social classes in society separated the art of the private career artist from folk art, thus forming two major art systems and two cultural heritages in China. The former was the communal art of the people and first came into being in prehistoric time; the latter was the art created by individual career artists and professionals. The parallel growth and mutual influences of these two types of art have been key in driving forward the mainstream of Chinese national art.

In terms of the conservation of national culture, the life of folk art is relatively stable. It represents the ideology of the community; the emotional and psychological characteristics of a nation throughout major periods in history. It is coexistent with national culture; it will not disappear as long as the community exists. Traditional folk art will, however, continue to grow and expand with the passage of time. Cross-cultural exchange and development will continually inject new life into folk art by bringing fresh materials and ideas. Its core, however—its cultural and philosophical origin, its Chinese cultural genes—will remain unchanged.

Chinese folk art has six basic features:

1. It is the art of the people and by the people. The creators are the vast majority of ordinary people as a group.

2. It is the art for the people. It is intended to meet the needs of their daily work, food, clothing, shelter and transportation; as well as their social life of festivals and ceremonies, of beliefs and taboos.

3. Its cultural implication and art forms are reprehensive of the world view of the community, their aesthetics, their emotional and psychological characteristics and national spirit. It reflects the system of philosophy, art and color composition in the original Chi-

nese culture. Some popular categories include paper-cutting; floury flower; dress and ornament; embroidery; dye and knitting; exorciser related masks and customs; painting; New Year picture; leather silhouette; puppet; toy; kite; paper folding and lighting art; folk theatrical mask; chess; puzzle; pottery; engraving; residential building; vehicle decoration; household appliance; etc.

4. It is a sector of Chinese parent art. Emerged in primitive society, Chinese folk art inherited the cultural tradition of national literature and art development throughout each and every period in a history of over several thousand years.

5. It is distinctively characterized by individual nationality and geographical region.

6. It is created with commonplace tools and indigent raw materials, characterized by rural natural economy of the region.

In sum, folk art is a unique sector among Chinese national art that enjoys the most popularity and with the richest resource of historical culture. It is directly embedded in people's every day life and best characterized by the geographical region it represents. It is a long-standing, signature art form of Chinese nation with 7,000–8,000 years of history and cultural progress going all the way back to primitive society. From the worship of nature, totem and ancestor; to the urban residence culture of modern capitalist commodity economy; the cultural identity of each historical period is recognizable in single piece of art work in some cases. It is truly a living fossil and a museum of national historical culture.

It is also necessary to address some misinterpretations in defining the concept of Chinese folk art:

Firstly, the notion to characterize Chinese folk art as "willful creations." I disagree. Willfulness can be found in Chinese paintings, art work and art style of career artists or professionals. It is not a definition of folk art. On the other hand, there is a variety of categories and diverse art styles in folk art. They are not all willful creations.

Secondly, the notion that "change of appearance" is the basic feature of Chinese folk art. I disagree. Change of appearance is not an exclusive technique employed in Chinese folk art. It is used by career artists too. In modern art, the style of changing appearance attempts to lead the trend of its time. The issue is not the appearance, or the change; it is to show what and how to change. The change of appearance in Chinese folk art is determined by the original Chinese philosophical comprehension, art system and its aesthetic view, apart from the art of Chinese professionals, and intrinsically different from the fashionable trend in modern western art.

Thirdly, learning from folk art, some professional artist created some art works with folk art style. They tend to characterize the work as folk art and label themselves as folk artists. It is actually a mis-conception that overlooked the fact that folk art is the art of the working class people. It is created by a group of massive laborers to serve the needs of their own social life. Even those art works did bear the artistic effect of folk art; it is still modern art by professional artists.

Fourthly, folk art differentiates from folk arts and crafts. The arts and crafts is a sector of folk art involving intensive craftsmanship, some are even consummate products. Folk art may not all have the same value or the craftsmanship as arts and crafts. They are two parts of the same category.

Lastly, folk art and folk custom art. Folk custom is the carrier of folk art. We speak of folk art from the angle of art; whereas folk custom art is in the view of the custom.

The Core of Chinese Folk Art

Folk social customs are the carriers of Chinese folk art which has numerous categories and a variety of art forms. However, despite all the categories and forms on the outside, the core lies within the basic cultural consciousness of the people and the original Chinese philosophy.

Life and Propagation
—an All-time Theme

To live and to continue life through propagation are the two in-
stinctive desires of humans. From birth, a person's first instinct is
to survive, then to live a long life. However, life and death are im-
mutable laws of nature. Therefore, they turned to seek perpetuity
after life, praying for longevity for the living, and perpetuity for
the dead. Since the eternity of life could only be achieved through
propagation, producing children and grandchildren to pass on life
from generation to generation became the ultimate goal. Thus,
human perception of propagation was the same as their perception of life itself. Propagation of people and harvesting of crops
were deemed as good fortune. In this way, fortune and longevity
became the basic cultural consciousness of the people, which was
also the main theme of folk art.

Chinese folk art and Chinese philosophy are unified in the belief
that *yin-yang* produces all living things on earth and all living things
stay alive through propagation. Originated in Chinese primitive
society, this was the philosophical explanation of human's perception of life and propagation. Chinese ancestor's philosophical conclusion was to "look at oneself up close and other creatures from
afar." Observing one's own life in this manner would lead to the
understanding of other living things on earth. This conclusion had
been the essential cultural understanding of the primitive art to
the folk art of the nation.

With the coming of property ownership and intellectual
development, the society began to be divided into the governing
class and the governed. Class society was established. The majority of material and intellectual valuables were disproportionately
accumulated in the upper classes where they created a more afflu-

Folk paper-cut "Lotus bearing seeds" (Zhenyuan, Gansu).

ent life style. To get a better life, the concept of profit came into the larger community. The previous cultural concept of "fortune and longevity" expanded into "fortune, longevity, and wealth." Together they formed the secular culture of folk art. This was especially true in areas that were more culturally and economically developed. Folk art with themes of fortune, longevity, and wealth became widespread. In areas more culturally enclosed with undeveloped communications and economy, the themes were still luck and longevity symbolized by life and propagation. Folk art papercut of "Lotus bearing seeds" implied life and propagation in the rural area of northern Shaanxi. On the other hand, in Tianjin where the economy was more developed and transportation had become convenient, New Year woodcut pictures became "Lotus bearing precious seeds" and "Five sons obtaining official promotion." To become official was to be in the position to obtain wealth.

Transitioning from a natural farming economy to a commodity economy meant that there was a need for profitable commodities.

With this change money became important. This evolution in the society brought about a change in the folk art. The "Tree of life" turned into a "Tree that shed coins" or a "Treasure bowl." The goal in life was no longer to gain basic survival. Life and propagation gradually faded and was replaced by symbols denoting a happy life and good fortune. For example, by combining two items such as a halberd (symbolizing favorable circumstances) and jade (symbolizing fulfillment of ones wishes) auspicious good fortune would replace the original concept of perpetual life. Having many

Folk paper-cut "The tree of life" (Ansai, Shaanxi).

children was symbolized with lotus in a vase. Another example to have every wish granted was expressed by combining two persimmons with jade. The persimmons were symbolic of having everything. The life view changed from simple propagation to living comfortably with extras. Looking at Chinese folk art through different times is like separating cultural layers at an archaeological site. Every shard carries the trace of the historical culture of its time.

From primitive society to the present day, the views of *yin-yang* and perpetual life have permeated all aspects of the social life and national culture of Chinese society. Chinese folk art reflects all of the basic philosophical concepts of the society. From my research of Chinese and world archaeological cultures, I have concluded that *yin-yang* and perpetual life view were the two key factors in opening up the database of Chinese cultural genes. In Western cultures, everything evolves around perpetual life. Whereas yin-yang was regarded as the essence of Chinese cosmic ontology, it was regarded as part of dialectical methodology in the west.

Symbols of Visual Objects

The art form of Chinese folk art is the visual image of the objects in the universe, according to the original Chinese philosophy.

In primitive society, human was on the weak side in the struggle against natural disasters. Animals with superman capability became supernatural or totem animals in the eyes of humans, for example, polygenetic animals like fish, toad and frog were regarded as female totem symbols from mother's body of earth and water. Animals that were difficult to conquer such as snake, tiger, ox, boar, bear, or with special capability such as flying birds and butterflies, or that ran fast on mountain peaks and precipices like antelope, were male totem symbols, same as the sky and the sun. Over the course of several thousand years, these symbols have been, and

A totem coiled snake on painted pottery unearthed from Taosi cultural relics (dated back 5,000 years) in Xiangfen, Shanxi, along middle-to-upper reaches of the Yellow River.

Folk paper-cut "Snake twining round a rabbit" (Ansai, Shaanxi), middle-to-upper reaches of the Yellow River.

Floury flower of "Wonton" (chaos) totem snake in Shilou, Shanxi, middle-to-upper reaches of the Yellow River.

One carving of tiger face totem from Yangshao Culture (dated back 6,000 years, kept at the Shaanxi Historical Museum).

Tiger totem cap, shoes and pillow for babies (Linyi, Shandong).

still are, used by people of various national background and geographical areas in their respective regional folk art.

In the prairie areas of northern China, the deer totem symbol worshipped by the people in remote antiquity is still a symbol in today's folk art of the prairie culture; and the pig and the dragon totem from Hongshan Culture originated in primitive society in Liaohe River basin are still feature symbols in the folk art of the region. The turtle, the snake, the fish and the frog totem from Yangshao Culture along the middle-upper stream of the Yellow

A hanging dish of tiger face totem as Patron Saint (Fengxiang, Shaanxi).

Hongshan Culture

Hongshan Culture derives its name from Hongshanhou Site, Chifeng, Inner Mongolia, where the first site of such culture was discovered. Mainly distributed southeast Inner Mongolia and west of Liaoning Province, it covers an area of 200,000 square kilometers. Existing around 5,000 or 6,000 years ago, Hongshan Culture lasted for 2,000 years. Hongshan Culture was at the peak development of Matriarchal clan society, which consisted of tribal groups bonded by maternal blood ties. The economic pattern was dominated by agriculture and supplemented with animal husbandry, fishery, and hunting. The handicraft industry reached a very high level. There appeared highly distinctive pottery decoration art and greatly developed jade-making techniques. The jade pig-dragon is the representative jade artifact of Hongshan Culture. Its curly body, highly-held snout, and flowing hair radiate a great sense of motion.

Birds playing around with fish in the mouth on painted pottery from Yangshao culture (dated back 6,000 years) unearth from Beishouling, Baoji, Shaanxi.

River were worshipped by the emperor tribe who idolized earth and land. East of Gansu to central Shaanxi plain, Fuxi, Yan Di and ancient Qiang ethnic group tribes worshipped tiger, ox and goat which were regarded as the same type of symbols as the sky and the sun. Lower stream of the Yangtze River was the region for Hemudu Culture and Ancient Yue tribal culture that worshipped the bird totem. Going north into Shangdong Province was also the bird totem from Dawenkou Culture and Longshan Culture; and midstream Yangtze River Chiyou Miao-Li tribal group was known for their ox totem in connection with the sky and the sun. The same went all the way to the upper stream of the Yangtze River. Regional totem symbols still prevail in today's folk art.

In ancient China, people connected natural animals with sky and earth, and with the theory of *yin-yang*. Animals in the yang group symbolized the sky and the sun. The unification of "*yang*" animal from the sky with "*yin*" animals of earth meant a connection of the sky and earth, or the unity of *yin-yang*. Among Chinese totem animals and legendary animals, the tiger, the ox, the goat, the bird, the bear, the boar, the dog and the rooster were

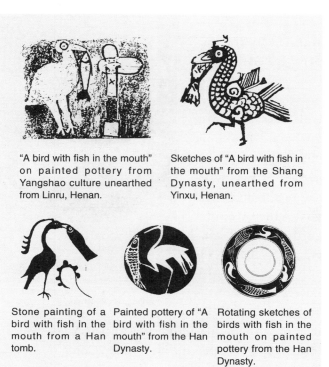

"A bird with fish in the mouth" on painted pottery from Yangshao culture unearthed from Linru, Henan.

Sketches of "A bird with fish in the mouth" from the Shang Dynasty, unearthed from Yinxu, Henan.

Stone painting of a bird with fish in the mouth from a Han tomb.

Painted pottery of "A bird with fish in the mouth" from the Han Dynasty.

Rotating sketches of birds with fish in the mouth on painted pottery from the Han Dynasty.

Hemudu Culture

Hemudu Culture is the Neolithic culture distributed in the lower reaches of the Yangtze River. Extant around 6,000 to 7,000 years ago, Hemudu Culture is named after the earliest excavated site in Hemudu Village, Yuyao, Zhejiang Province. The social economy of Hemudu Culture centered on rice cultivation. There was also animal husbandry, collecting, fishing and hunting. The relics of a large number of stilt houses were found at the site. Also discovered at the site were remains of rice, which were determined as cultivated by humans. Domesticated animals included pigs, dogs, and water buffalos. The artifacts are mainly wood implements and bone articles, among which there is China's earliest wood ornament "wood-carved fish" as well as large quantities of textile tools.

of the sky and *yang* group; the dragon, the snake, the turtle, the fish and the frog were *yin* group and symbols of earth and water. The dragon, with his head on earth but mating in heaven, was a totem of both worlds. (Dragon was originally an animal of earth and water, but later went to heaven to become the king, and phoenix, an animal in heaven was the queen.) This is rather unique. For example, dragon, being an earth and water totem symbol, later became a cultural symbol of the entire nation in the confluence of multiple national cultures. People integrated the dragon into their own totem animal which turned into the dragon with a boar head in Liaohe River basin; or the dragon with a tiger head in

Dawenkou Culture

Dawenkou Culture is the typical culture of patriarchal clan society in the later phase of Neolithic Age. With Mount Tai as the center, Dawenkou Culture covered an area that stretched from the shore of Yellow Sea in the east to the Luxi Plain in the west and from the southern shore of the Bohai Sea in the north to today's Huaibei area of Jiangsu Province in the south. There were also a small number of such remains discovered in Anhui and Henan provinces. Dawenkou Culture derived its name from the first place of such sites—Dawenkou, Tai'an, Shandong Province. The discovery of Dawenkou Culture has pushed back 2,000 years the history of the primeval culture in the lower reaches of Yellow River from the Longshan Culture over 4,000 years ago. The graves of the later phase of Dawenkou Culture show the joint burial of husband and wife and the co-burial of husband, wife, and children, which marks the ending of the matriarchal society in which only the mother was known to the children and the beginning of patriarchal society.

the middle-upper stream of the Yellow River; the dragon with a bird head in middle-lower stream of the Yellow River and the Yangtze River; and the dragon with an ox head in middle-upper stream of the Yangtze River. It is also quite common to see "fish with a tiger head" or "fish with a rooster head" in Chinese folk art. When two animals are combined into one, it was a cultural symbol that heaven and earth connect, male and female mate.

Embroidery costume "Dragon with an ox head" (Two dragons playing a pearl) (Taijiang, Guizhou).

Other example like "rooster holding a fish in the mouth" and "bird holding a fish in the mouth" also implied the connection of heaven and earth, yin and yang. It was a cultural code originated in the communal philosophy in primitive society.

Another symbol in Chinese folk art was a pair of animals on each side of the tree of life. This was a common design in silk weaving pictures from the Silk Road. In the Ancient Babylon culture of primitive society, a tree meant the tree of life, and it was guarded by the two animals, one on each side. However, when such totem was introduced to China, the two animals from the opposite side were given a philosophical nature as *yin* and *yang*, male and female. The totem symbols in Chinese primitive society were the paired fish, toads, snakes, tigers, deer and birds, all paired up as male and female, *yin* and *yang*, or animals of earth and the sky.

The planetary paired fish, toads, deer, goats, and birds revolving in the sky in primitive and folk art are philosophical symbols which unified in the theory of *yin-yang* and perpetual life. Such philosophical and cultural implications were revealed in folk art designs in which two totem animals facing each other, with a symbolic sun up

Longshan Culture

Longshan Culture broadly refers to the culture of the later phase of Neolithic Age. In this culture both bronze and stone implements were used. Named after Longshan Town, Zhangqiu, Shandong Province, where it was first discovered, Longshan Culture existed about 4,350–3,950 years ago. It was distributed in the middle and lower reaches of Yellow River, like the provinces of Shandong, Henan, Shanxi, and Shaanxi.

Paper-cut for window flower—"A fish with a rooster head" (Ansai, Shaanxi).

Paper-cut for window flower—"A bird with fish in the mouth" (Shaanxi).

Embroidery curtain "Dragon with a phoenix head" (Two dragons playing a pearl) (Songtao, Guizhou).

Pillow showing a fish with a tiger head (Jishan, Shanxi).

above in the middle, such as "Two dragons playing with a ball," "Two phoenixes facing toward the sun," or with a symbol of life in the middle in "The tree of life and a pair of deer," "The tree of life with a pair of goats," or "The tree of life with a pair of monkeys," etc.

The pattern of two animals revolving in opposite directions implies the revolution of the universe and continuation of life. Common patterns are rotating fish in pairs, triples or quadruples; or rotating birds. Sometimes, the fish or the revolving fish are painted on the bottom or the lower part of a dish, a metaphor for mother's body of the universe, to symbolize the revolution of earth; or on the upper portion or the edge of the utensils, to symbolize the revolution of the sky.

Among the legendary animals, proliferous animal was regarded as god of propagation, such as rat. As a folk proverb goes, rat being "the smallest in size, but the biggest among the twelve animals of earthly branches." Cultural symbols implying proliferation are shown in "Rat eating pumpkin," "Rat eating grape" and "Rat stealing oil" (oil container as mother's body for propagation). Theme paper-cut and woodcut New Year picture "Rat marry off a daughter," came from the legend that the rat, god of propagation, marries off a daughter every year on "The Human Day," the 7th of first lunar month. Rabbit, also proliferous, is another god of propagation in "Rabbit eating cabbage," "Rabbit coiled by a snake," an image of totem snake protecting and nurturing the newborns.

Sketches of a pair of revolving fish on painted pottery from Yangshao Culture, Banpo (dated back 6,000 years).

Insects with arms and legs spreading out from the center body are visual images of the sun in Chinese folk art works, such as crab, spider, scorpion, beetle, centipede, etc. They were originally symbols of the sun in ancient Egypt and ancient Babylon, and made its way to China via the Silk Road as early as primitive time. In west China along the Silk Road, eastern Gansu and central Shaanxi plain area, every year on the Dragon Boat Festival, people still wear these animal figures on their vests, tan tops and hand bags as talismans, or symbols of patron saint. People call them five poisonous creatures nowadays, but they were actually old time legendary animals regarded as the sun god. The "Five poisonous creatures" are not supposed to get on body wear; however, it is acceptable to wear them in the chest or on the back for safeguard. One of the toughest two periods for Chinese to survive against natural environment is, for one, the Summer Solstice (Late June in the Gregorian calendar), the longest day in a year and in the dead heat of season, with pestilence running rampant, threatening human lives. To invite these little sun animals out and wear

"Revolving birds and fish" on white porcelain basin from the Liao Dynasty (dated back 1,000 years).

"Three revolving fish" on blue and white porcelain bowl (Chengxian County, Shaanxi).

Paper-cut "A pair of deer and a pair of crane facing the Tree of Life" (Deer and crane welcome the arrival of spring) (Zhenyuan, Gansu).

Paper-cut "Rats eating grape" (Yichuan, Shaanxi).

Paper-cut "Rat marrying off a daughter" (Qianyang, Shaanxi).

Paper-cut "Rabbits eating cabbage" (Ansai, Shaanxi).

Decorative talisman "Crab curbing the five poisonous creatures."

them as talismans is to use poison as an antidote against poison. The winter Solstice (late December in the Gregorian calendar) is the coldest day and longest night in a year, a time ghosts and spirits run around.

It is custom to put out symbols of rooster, another sun god, homophonic with "Double chicks" and "Baby with coiled hair" with double coils and a rooster on each; or having roosters all over her body; to keep away ghosts and evil spirits. This is also originated in the primitive culture along the two Babylon rivers. In ancient times, it went west to Europe, and east to China. When mingled with Chinese culture, it became a symbol of the communal culture in Chinese folk art ever since.

Human body as the celestial body—Not just totem and legendary animals are taken as symbols of the universe by Chinese folk art, human body is also an entity symbolizing integration of heaven and earth.

Chinese emphasizes on the head. Likening human head to the universe, the top head is the sky; the two eyes are the moon and the sun; the chin is earth, and the mouth is the uterus of mother's body, the source of life

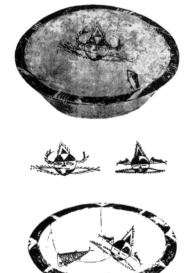

"Human face with fish in the mouth" on painted pottery from Yangshao Culture dated back 6,000 years.

Folk paper-cut "Human face with fish in the mouth."

propagation; the nose is the tree of life stretching from heaven to earth. There were numerous such illustrations in the primitive culture. "A human face with a fish in the mouth" from Yangshao Culture of Banpo, Xi'an; the binary eyes in Hemudu Culture; a mouth with protruding teeth from Hunan Gaomiao Culture; were a few examples.

Appliance and utensils as the universe—the philosophical concept of "looking at oneself up close and other creatures from afar" in Chinese folk art perceives the objects protruding upward as a life code for *yang*, reaching out to the sky and the sun; and the hollow objects as symbol of *yin*, the uterus of mother's body. Utensils like a bowl, a container, a bottle, a pot, and a dish are mother's body of the universe. The center is the uterus; the opening is the round sky and the bottom is earth, forming a complete universal symbol with three key elements, the sky, earth and the people. Totem animals or earth and heaven animals of *yin-yang* nature are often painted on the center part where the uterus is, such as mating

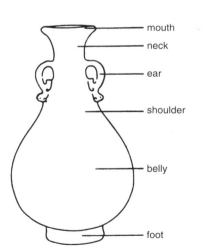

Household appliance reflecting ancient Chinese views of mother's body of the universe.

Sketches on bronze ware from the Shang Dynasty.

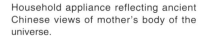

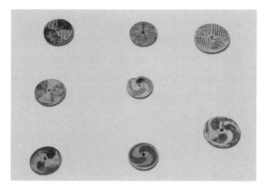

Rotating symbols on a spinning wheel from the Chinese primitive society of 5,500 years ago, unearthed from Qujialing, Hubei.

of two tigers; mating of two fish; or a pair of tigers with one head; a goat and a sheep sharing a common head; two dragons with one head; or a pair of dragons on a tiger head; implying connection between earth and the sky, *yin-yang* and perpetual life. From the porcelains of primitive society, to the bronze appliance of the Shang (1600–1046 BC) and Zhou (1046–256 BC) slave society; and the appliance and utensils in the imperial palaces of each dynasty or used by the ordinary people; were all based on the same concept. Every two-piece item that had an upper and lower part was interpreted as the combination of heaven and earth, the union of male and female. For example, a tea pot with a lid, the pot was mother's body, earth and the lid was the sky and the sun; art work "Buckled bowl," the upper lid is the sky and the bowl is earth.

In the culture of primitive society, things that rotate were symbols of life moving in cycles of perpetuity. The earliest geometry symbol was a rotating Chinese character "Wan," drawn from the visual image of a manifold on a spinning wheel.

In the world of nature, the sun is a lumi-

Revolving *Yin-Yang* fish symbol on a stone grinder used by the Chinese people (Yanchuan, Shaanxi).

Flower petals for sun rays on pottery vase from Dawenkou Culture (dated back 6,000 years).

nous body. In Chinese folk art, plants with flower petals radiating from the center become a symbol of the sun, such as chrysanthemum, rose, peony and sun flower. The earliest plant used to symbolize the sun was on painted pottery from the 6,000-year-old Yangshao Culture and Dawenkou Culture.

After Buddhism was introduced to China, the image of lotus flower appeared in the primitive culture and folk art. Being a water plant, lotus was a symbol of water and earth. In folk art, peony was often a metaphor for yang or male; while lotus was for yin or female. However, it was interchangeable. "Phoenix playing around a peony" in which the peony meant to be a female; in another case, "Lotus in a vase," the vase was mother's body of the universe and lotus was the sun flower that could reach the sky.

From the primitive culture to folk art, most of the images drawn from the visual plants were proliferous by nature, such as melon, fruits and vegetables, symbolizing mother's body of the universe that gave life to humans and all living things on earth. First of such images was a gourd. A good number of gourd bottles were seen in Yangshao Culture. They all had the same design

Painting by a farmer: Human ancestor in mother's body of the universe (Yijun, Shaanxi).

with an upward nozzle open to the sky as mother's body of the universe. Others images like pumpkin, grape, pear, cabbage, etc. were also symbols of propagation from proliferous mother's body.

Totems

Baby with coiled hair—A ball flower paper-cut "Baby with coiled hair" is very popular among the folks on the Loess Plateau along the Yellow River basin. In the center of the ball is this baby with coiled hair, who is a patron saint and god of propagation on the Loess Plateau. Wearing a hair style with double coils upward to the sky, and holding a pair of fish in both arms, she assumes a squatting posture as if giving birth. The lower part of her body is a pair of scissors pointing downward to imply the nature of male or *yang*, which, corresponding with her hair coils implies that she is hermaphroditic god of the universe. Scissors is *yang* by nature, a sharp tool that keeps away evil spirits and disasters. As a folk proverb goes: "Awl and scissors drive away the five poisonous creatures. " Some folk art works make the eyes of god as the sun. The two breasts are the two eyes of a cicada, a legendary animal of propagation, to symbolize a continued and never ending posterity. On each side are symbols of "Sheng" (a music instrument, hegemony of "birth" in Chinese), or lotus flowers. "Sheng" is "birth" and lotus is a proliferous symbol with male nature. A local folk proverb goes: "When lotus and sweet osmanthus growing out of a bucket, we have sons, daughters and nephews; when golden cicada blow-

A ball flower paper-cut "Baby with coiled hair."

Folk paper-cut—a pair of fish with human faces (Zhenyuan, Gansu).

Folk paper-cut—paired fish doll with coiled hair (Qingyang, Gansu).

ing 'Sheng,' family posterity never ends." "A ripe persimmon bears eight precious 'Sheng (kids),' and a lotus plants the seeds." In this art work, god of the universe holds *yin* and *yang* two fish, one in each hand, with their tails connecting in a continuous character "Wan" without breaking up, implying a never ending prosperity and continued posterity. In the lower part of the picture are two geometry symbols of Ruyi (good luck), and a legendary rabbit holding grass in the mouth. Rabbit, hegemony of "spit kids," is god of proliferation. Two rabbits with double Ruyi have the meaning giving birth to a succession of sons one after another. A wedding song used by the people of the Loess Plateau has "double walnuts and double jujubes, double sons and daughters chasing around. A good son is expected to grow up wearing cap and blue gown (to become an official); and a daughter is to be capable with her hands." With the art of paper-cut, "every cut has a meaning of its own" said the grandmother who made this art work of multi-lateral, collective symbols and cultural codes with the theme of life and propagation. If a paper-cut for window decoration could be a tourist book of northern Shaanxi, "Baby with coiled hair" would be an orchestra of the paper-cut art. It is actually a transformed version of "Double fish with human faces" on 600-year-old painted pottery from the Yangshao Culture of Xi'an.

Paper-cut "paired fish dolls" from the Loess Plateau of Gansu Province has two *yin-yang* fish one on each side. It shares the same cultural implication and art form as "*Yin-yang* fish," and "Baby with coiled hair." In Luochuan, Shaanxi Province, it is in the form of a paired snake with coiled hair, and paired dragon with coiled hair. In Chinese folk art, fish, snake (dragon) and baby girl are related and interchangeable.

Paired fish with human face on painted pottery from Banpo— In Shaanxi, Shanxi and Gansu area, a similar image as "Baby with coiled hair" is the "Paired fish with human faces" on painted pottery from Yangshao Culture of 6,000 years ago unearthed in Banpo. People tend to connect this with the fishing and hunting life style of primitive society. As some argued, the sketches on each side were symbols of a fish net. The painting showed only the heads, the interpretation went on as: two fish nets were set open, and two people were in the water. Their feet being in the water were left out. It was implied that their hands were busy catching fish under the water. By closing in from two opposite sides, they made the fish running into the net. Their half closed eyes were a sub-conscious facial look when focused on catching fish. It seems to me, however,

An eight diagrams symbol on the edge of a painted pottery showing a pair of revolving fish and a human face with closed eyes as supernatural creatures from Yangshao Culture, Banpo.

Sketches of a pair of fish with human face on a painted pottery from Yangshao Culture, Banpo type.

the creators of the art work in primitive society always tried to convey the original Chinese philosophy through cultural symbols and codes that were accepted by the community. Without the knowledge of original Chinese philosophy, it would be impossible to decode their symbols, nor to interpret Chinese archaeology art or folk art. Take fish for example, the paired fish created in the art work was not the fish in their natural being. It was *yin-yang* fish symbols. The two fish on painted pottery rotating towards opposite direction were *yin-yang* fish revolving around the sky, a conceptual symbol of perpetual life.

Human face with paired fish—Corresponding with paper-cut "*Yin-yang* fish" and "Baby with coiled hair," "Paired fish with human face" on painted pottery symbolizes the first ancestor, god of the universe. Looking at this image, god has one eye open, and the other eye closed. Apparently, they are not the natural but conceptual eyes. With god of the universe, the open eye is the sun, the day, and *yang*; the closed eye is the moon, the night, and *yin*.

It is common practice in Chinese folk art to liken eye to the sun and the moon. In folk art painting created by the women in northern Shaanxi, all human faces are round-eyed, same as the eyes of the tiger. Their eye balls are always in the center of the white unsheltered by eye lids. It is believed that a closed eye is the moon and an open eye is the sun. Therefore, eyes should be painted bright and shining. To me, that might also be a cultural comprehension from the primitive clans.

Fish net—A widely used code in Chinese folk art is fish net. From the primitive society to today, this ever-popular symbol of perpetual life bears a cultural heritage shared by all people on earth. For thousands of years, it has been a sign of auspice and good luck, or Ruyi (wishes being granted) in every way. It is also known as the code of the Eight Diagrams. The transformed patterns and names of this code further enriched the implications it carried. The popular "China Net" being worn as an adornment in the chest or

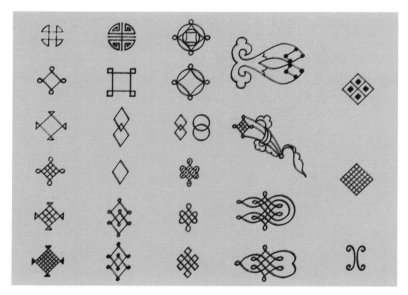

Various forms of eight diagrams in China.

hung in bedrooms today is from the very code of the fish net. On painted pottery "Human face holding a fish in the mouth" from Yangshao Culture, the starting end of the fish net sketch was a "+" and an "x." "+" was the graphic sign of the sun, but "x" was the code for a rotating sun and a revolving earth. The first sign was a square, a double square or a chequer code; the second sign was a diamond and the net veins; that is the fish net symbol of life.

Over thousands of years, these two symbols and a variety of their extended forms have maintained a lasting popularity in West Asia, China, even around the globe, embedded in all aspects of social life and folk customs in daily food, clothing, shelter and transportation, custom rituals and ceremonies; holidays and festivities, beliefs and taboos. Stone painting from the Han

"Fish net" on painted pottery and paired fish with human faces from Yangshao Culture, Banpo.

Chinese New Year festivity in Shaanxi—going through zigzag diagram in nine tunes.
Upper: A plane view of a zigzag diagram.
Middle: Arranging the stage for nine tune game.
Lower: Going through nine tune game.

tombs in Shandong Province with a lark holding a red book in the mouth was a fish net symbol same as the one on the painted pottery from Banpo. "The treasure toad" and "A snake twining round nine eggs" among the folks in northern Shaanxi; the "Eight diagrams" and "A toad over a square" from Hebei; "Two snakes twining around nine eggs" (meaning dragon laying nine eggs) on baby's pillow case in Weihe Valley; and the popular "China net" on the market today; are all transformed patterns from the fish net symbol. Even "Yangko," the popular Chinese New Year folk dance loved by the people in northern Shaanxi, is tuned in steps of nine squares and eight diagrams derived from the fish net symbol.

The same symbol on rock carving from ancient Tuyuhun in west China's Buerda mountain area is still a popular sign of good fortune often seen on each side of buildings or tents in southern Gansu, Qinghai and part of Tibet where inhabitants are largely Qiang ethnic groups. After Buddhism got into China from India, this symbol became one of the eight symbolic treasures of Buddhist to cherish across China.

Dancing dolls on painted pottery

and paper-cut "Five Fairies"—A representative work of Yangshao Culture from the Neolithic Age was the dancing dolls on painted pottery unearthed from Sunjiazhai, Daotong County, Qinghai Province, in 1973. The main part of the picture was three sets of five dolls, hand-in-hand. It was named "Dancing dolls", and interpreted as depiction of a dancing scene by some scholars. However, when I showed it to some grandmothers in northern Shaanxi, they called it "Fairies from five paths." They were fairies of east, north, south, west and the center. It is a popular paper-cut in northern Shaanxi used in reviving spirits in local customs. When kids get sick, the family would make "Fairies from five paths" paper-cut in yellow paper, pick it up with a willow twig and stroke it over the sick body while mumbling something. Then, burn it and spread the ashes into a bowl of water; take the clothes of the kid to a

Paper-cut "Baby dolls with linked hands."

Sketches of "Dancing dolls" on painted pottery from Majiayao Culture (dated back 5,000 years).

Paper-cut "Fairies from five paths," the saints who expel diseases (Yanchuan, Shaanxi).

five-way crossing to spill the water there; calling the name of the kid on the way to and back from the crossing. People also hang "Five fairies" paper-cut on the lintel to keep evils away from the house. The number of the dolls can be in five, seven, three or nine, always an odd number as the "*yang*" nature. Other times the dolls are made of pumpkin seeds and black beans, as "Pumpkin seeds dolls," to be pasted inside the room.

Social Context of Chinese Folk Art

The carriers of folk art are folk social customs. The original philosophy and visual image based on folk art is the product of the Chinese community and has become in-grown in people's social life. Its all time theme of life and propagation meets the needs in different aspects of life, displaying its beauty in a variety of colorful ways.

The Social Context of Folk Arts

Birth

What is the theme of human birth? First it is to know where life comes from; and then to wish that the newborn grows up healthy and strong.

Human life comes from mother's body of the universe, which the Chinese believe is as primeval as pigeon eggs, and from mother's body of totem animals. Therefore, it is customary to give chicken eggs, which are known as the "red egg" in Hunan and Hubei in the Yangtze River valley. People also paste paper-cut "The tree of life" in bright red color on the red eggs as good-wish for the newborn. In the Yellow River basin where flour is a staple food, people make steamed bread, symbolizing the domed universe. Inside the bread are red beans implying that a new life has been conceived; "Wonton" steamed bread are made with two curly twists, implying the unification of *yin-yang* that creates life on earth.

The "red egg" from the maternal family sent on the first full month of a new born, with paper-cut "evergreen tree" pasted on it, a folk custom along the Yangtze River valley (Taojiang, Hubei).

The "Wonton" gift bread with red bean inside from the maternal family celebrating the first full month of a new born, a folk custom along the Yellow River reaches (Huaxian County, Shaanxi).

Floury flower dragon with a tiger head and a fish tail, carrying all living things in the universe on its back (Houma, Shanxi).

A pair of "fish pillow," a gift from relatives of the maternal family (Zhengning, Gansu).

"Crawling baby" pillow from the maternal family. On the right is a porcelain pillow from the Song Dynasty.

In Shanxi and Shaanxi, birth bread is called "Wonton," or "Grain twist."

Human life comes from mother's body of totem animals, god of propagation. In areas where people worship legendary animals or totem animals like the turtle, the snake, the fish and the frog; and in places where supernatural power becomes personalized in "Baby with coiled hair;" birth presents from the maternal family are pillow case with patterns of a paired fish (*yin-yang*), or a paired turtles and a paired frogs. There are also embroidery patterns called "Crawling baby with coiled hair." This is very similar to the design on the porcelain pillow from northern China in Song (960–1279), Yuan (1206–1368), Ming (1368–1644) and Qing (1616–1911) dynasties. It is interesting to note that a diamond shaped symbol like a female uterus is placed in the center among the animals, implying that the new baby comes from mother's body of legendary animals or god of propagation. In areas where people worship tiger, the gifts are "Wonton" steamed bread painted with patterns like a snake with a tiger head (the sky) and a fish tail (the earth); with the entire living world on its back. At birth, one month anniversary, and the first birthday, the baby sleeps on a "tiger head" pillow; wearing a tiger cap and a pair of tiger head shoes and a tiger head undergarment. He looks just like a descendant of the tiger totem family.

Easting floury sheep (Cixian County, Hebei).

In areas where people worship sheep, it is popular to make "floury sheep" bread. In Hebei and Shanxi area, it is two sheep sharing a common head; or sheep head with fish tail; implying the unity of *yin-yang*; or a herd of three sheep to mark a new beginning of life. Each year, the "Sheep Day" festival in Cixian County, Hebei, at the end of wheat harvest season draws large crowds. Relatives from the maternal family make big baskets of "floury sheep" bread for their daughter's baby. Those who live far away come on bikes or tractors. A large herd of floury sheep are displayed in front of the baby. The presentation usually includes a big round Wonton jujubes sandwich bread in the center, symbolizing the universe, surrounded by paired sheep with one head (*yin-yang* sheep) and a huge herd of baby sheep. The first three years after the baby is born are given big sheep, second and third year are large-to-medium and medium in size, and the subsequent years will be small sheep until he/she gets married.

In today's folk custom, the 12 animals of earthly branches that differentiate the year of birth still hold a wide-spread popularity. People take it seriously about the nature of the animal for the year they were born, and often wear a jade adornment of their own animal on birthdays. This too is an extension of the totem animal culture from primitive society to modern life. The same is true with the concept of the "descendant of dragon" in China.

Wedding Ceremonies

Traditional wedding is meant for the union of a male and a female, *yin and yang*, which lead to human propagation and perpetual life. The folk art works on custom wedding ceremony bear distinctive features on the theme.

Fish, being a proliferous legendary animal, is often used to symbolize having multiple children. A *yin-yang* paired fish became a cultural code in Chinese folk art works.

At wedding ceremony, paper-cut "Fish playing around lotus,"

A large-scale "Happy baby" ball flower paper-cut, pasted in the center of the cave window at wedding ceremonies (Ansai, Shaanxi).

"Wonton" gift floury flower "A tiger with an egg in the mouth" (Huaxian County, Shaanxi).

"Fish biting lotus," "Lotus bearing seeds" and "Happy dolls" (baby with coiled hair holding a pair of fish) are pasted on the ceiling of the bridal chamber. In northern Shaanxi, red or green paper-cutting of "Baby with coiled hair holding a pair of fish" in a big ball flower design is pasted on the center of the cave window. They are

"Wonton" floury flower from the maternal family (Huaxian County, Shaanxi).

Undergarment featuring "Carp with an open cut" embroidered by the bride for her husband (Luochuan, Shaanxi).

called "revolving flower," as the revolving sky. The lower and middle part of the cave window is usually a lattice window in 36 counts. A large totem animal paper-cut (a tiger, a sheep or a deer) is over the middle four lattice; each corner lattice has a corner flower; the rest space are filled with colorful paper-cuts like "Buckled bowls," "Paired fish," "Fish playing around lotus," "Lotus bearing babies," "Rat eating pumpkins," "Squirrel eating grape," "Monkey eating peach," "Rabbit eating cabbage," "Golden pheasant visiting lotus flower," etc., making up a diamond square shaped "36 lattice window of clouds." The colorful paper-cuttings against the white window paper liner definitely add a delightful atmosphere. In here, rat, squirrel, rabbit and golden pheasant are male; and lotus flower, pumpkin, grape, cabbage and peach are female. Putting animals and plants implies combining male and female for multiplication.

Male monkey (symbolic of the husband) made by the bride and to be placed at the bottom of her bridal suitcase (Baoji, Shaanxi).

Porcelain "Happy baby," god of propagation, placed at the bottom of the bridal suitcase by the bride to take to the groom's house (Yuxian County, Henan).

In the upper and middle reaches of the Yellow River, gift bread for wedding ceremony from the maternal family is a round bread made of two connecting fish, or a tiger head on a dragon body with a fish tail, with a world of living things plugged on the back. In Huaxian County, Shaanxi Province, the wedding bread is a "High rise bread platter" with a reed cylinder in the center as if connecting to the sky; and paired fish stuck on very layer from bottom up, such as a paired fish sharing one tiger head or a sheep head; a paired dragons with a tiger head; or a fish tail with a phoenix head. The top layer is a treasure bottle and a happy baby, a symbol of wealth and more children. At the wedding, two "High rise bread platters" are placed on each side of the table where the bride and the groom bow to the sky, to earth and to each other. It is quite a scene.

In Shaanxi, Shanxi and eastern Gansu, a custom wedding embroidery is a hand made red undergarment, showing a fish (the bride) with an open cut on her body (a female uterus). It is part of the dowry as a gift from the bride to her groom. Other embroideries include male and female animals of proliferous nature; hanging ornaments of flowers and fruits; or a "Needle holder," a "Needle toad," as gifts for the female in-laws to show off bride's craftsmanship.

A custom in the monkey totem tribal culture in Henan is for the bride to embroider a male monkey, symbolic of her husband, and hide it at the bottom of the suitcase to take with her to the husband's family on the wedding day. A secret porcelain "Happy baby," with female coiled hair but a male body, is placed under the bed sheet on the wedding night. It is meant to be crushed during intercourse, a prayer for more children. Traditional porcelain "Happy baby" is still being made today at a porcelain cellar known for manufacturing the Song Dynasty porcelain in Yuxian county of Henan Province.

Funerals and Memorial Services

The keynote for funeral and memorial service is spiritual eternity and continuation of life after death. This is also the main theme of Chinese folk art works on the subject. Death at old age is a normal course of life referred to as "passing away" or "return to heaven," which means back to mother's body of the universe. Wedding and funeral are "red and white happy events" in Chinese culture.

Wonton gift bread "Supreme worship goodies" for funeral and memorial services (Luochuan, Shaanxi).

By social customs, steamed bread for funeral and memorial service is the "old bread." It is the same dome-shaped universe as the one for birth, but without the red bean inside. The elimination of the multiplication symbol reflects the philosophical comprehension that life comes from the universe through birth, and goes back through death.

Funeral "Wonton" bread is a three-layer round cake with a circle of red jujubes on each layer. It is the same shape and size as the Chinese New Year bread except that a cypress twig is placed on the top to symbolize eternity for the dead.

Embroidery works for funeral service include a pillow with a "Rooster to call for the spirit" or the "old pillow" which has a girl and a boy on each side, and a pair of "old shoes" which has embroidery "Lotus flower," metaphorical of water and earth. Old pillow and old shoes are likened to heaven and earth. When the spirit of the dead connects to heaven and earth, it reaches eternity.

Yunnan Dai ethnic group's "Ladder to the sky," hanging at the sky column in the temple at funeral service (Xishuangbanna, Yunnan).

Double rooster pillow for the deceased person at funeral services (Qianyang, Shaanxi)

Origami for funeral service is a full series by itself in folk paper-cut. People cut or fold all kinds of imaginary personal articles with paper for the person who passed away to use in another world to be incriminated with the body. Each article had a special symbolic feature. In Yunnan, memorial service of Dai ethnic group had a 9-meter high "Ladder to heaven" hanging to the column inside the temple so the spirit of the dead could rise to heaven. The ladder was decorated with embroidery symbols of sky reaching tower, legendary animals and the tree of life.

Modern funeral and memorial service have changed the old custom in many ways. Origami and other imitation articles are no longer used. Wreath is used for sacrificial burials, which is seen as sun flower; and instead of making paper posts, people now use ever green cypress twig to symbolize the tree of life. It is a different art form, but the same cultural implication.

Folk Arts and Festivities

Chinese New Year

Chinese New Year, also known as the Spring Festival, is the biggest holiday in China. Recorded in *Li Ji* (Book of Rites), Chinese

Scene of Chinese New Year festivity inside the cave in northern Shaanxi.

Papercut for window decoration at Chinese New Year (Weixian County, Hebei).

New Year is the time when "the vapours of heaven descend and those of the earth ascend. Heaven and earth are in harmonious co-operation. All plants bud and grow." This summarizes the main features of folk art works on Chinese New Year, which are heaven and earth, *yin* and *yang*, propagation and harvest.

Chinese New Year window decoration usually bears the same implication as for wedding ceremonies. The best I have seen is the paper-cut on the cave windows on the Loess Plateau. On New Year's Eve, people put on brand new white window liner. Above the crossbar of the cave window is considered the sky. On the center of the crossbar is a large ball flower of "Baby with coiled hair holding a

pair of fish," is known as "Revolving flower" indicating that life revolves around the sky. Below the crossbar is the 36 window lattice. A totem animal (a tiger or a deer) takes the middle four lattice, and other window decorations fill the rest to form a diamond square design with end flowers on four corners. It is similar to the "Thirty-six window lattice of clouds" on wedding occasions, or the "Eight diagrams window." Themes of those paper-cuts include "Two dragons playing with a ball;" "Two phoenixes playing

Chinese New Year paper-cut on the door curtain and woodcut New Year picture of door god (Tancheng, Shandong).

Papercut to worship kitchen god at Chinese New Year (Yanchuan, Shaanxi).

Woodcut Chinese New Year picture to worship water well god (Fengxiang, Shaanxi).

around a peony;" "A golden clock over a frog;" "A deer and a crane;" "A snake twining round a rabbit;" "A vulture catching a rabbit;" "A dragon, a tiger and a vulture;" "Lion playing with a silk ball;" "A rooster holding a fish in the mouth;" "A rat bit open the sky;" "A bowl of Pomegranate;" "Buckled bowl in the shape of two frogs;" or of two fish, two tigers or two rats, "Fairy fish vase;" "Paired tiger vase;" "The Eight diagrams fish;" "Deer head;" etc. There are also a variety of paper-cuts with the theme of life and propagation: "A snake twining round nine eggs;" "Treasure toad;" "A pair of toad;" "Frog carrying a rock." It is a colorful picture of a legendary animal kingdom with birds flying, fish jumping, people laughing and horse soaring. Inside the cave, the *kang* is decorated with "Border flowers," across the dish rack is a row of "Dish rack clouds," and in the center of the ceiling is a large ball flower of "Phoenix playing around peony," and on the lintel is "Baby holding hands" or "Baby of sun flower seed."

In Shandong, the lower stream of the Yellow River, it is a whole different taste. The main subject of Chinese New Year paper-cut is the flower of life which grows high from a water pot or a fish bowl. Paper-cuts of the flower of life in a water vase, or the tree of life in a water pot, are pasted across the lintel. Similar paper-cut is also popular in northern Jiangsu, south of the Yellow River, all the way to the Yangtze River valley.

Nowadays urban residents like to paste Chinese New Year pa-

Woodcut Chinese New Year picture of "An armored horse" (Jianchuan, Yunnan).

Woodcut New Year picture "Sparrow marrying off a daughter" (Mianzhu, Sichuan).

per-cut character "Fu" (good fortune) upside, as "Fu dao" (good fortune arrives). Actually, the diamond square of upside down character "Fu" was meant to be a rotating symbol for perpetual life.

In Inner Mongolia, Chinese New Year door-god paper-cut is a pair of deer or a pair of roosters. In central Shaanxi, it is two tigers, and in Henan, two monkeys, or cows, or two babies with coiled hair riding a golden cow. These paper-cuts are made with yellow glossy paper, a common way to pray for patronage from the totem or legendary animals for family safety and keeping away evil spirits and disasters.

Chinese New Year is the "beginning of a year, everything starts fresh and gay." Every household changes a new woodcut of New Year picture. Polytheism that has been widely accepted by Chinese folks believes that every living creature has a power of its own. Such belief can be seen in some of the art works too. New Year picture featuring all types of gods are put out at Chinese New Year time for safeguard. On the 23rd of the twelfth lunar month is to worship the cooking stove, replacing a year old woodcut of "stove god" with a new one for the New Year. Pasted on the two door leaves are two famous warriors from the Tang Dynasty (618–907), door gods Shen Tu and Yu Lei, carrying reed ropes ready to kill any approaching demons. On the shrine by the door steps is god of land; in the yard are gods from ten directions; above the stove is god of wealth; and by the well is god of the well. In Yunnan, Yi and Bai ethnic groups culture has over 100 different images of gods for safeguard, each having a designated function.

The 7th of the first Lunar month is the "Human Day," the day the rat, god of propagation, marring off a daughter. Women would hide their basket of needlework to avoid being bitten by the rat. Big paper-cut "Rat marrying off a daughter" can be seen on the wall in every household on the Human Day. In other areas where birds are worshipped, like Sichuan, it is the "Sparrow marring off a daughter."

The 15th of the first lunar month is the Lantern Festival. Every household folds paper lanterns in a square or a diagram shape, fully decorated with colorful paper-cuts. Types of the lanterns vary from geographically related legendary animals to geometry symbols of life and propagation, such as "The moon lantern;" "Baby with coiled hair lantern;" "The eight diagrams lantern," to name a few.

"The moon lantern" (Longxian County, Gansu).

In the south of Yangtze River valley, between 1st–15th of the first lunar month, people have large gatherings to invite, dance for, and send off exorcists. It starts with

"Baby with coiled hair" lantern (Yanchuan, Shaanxi).

The Chinese New Year outdoor gathering in the suburban in the Miao village of northern Guizhou (Chishui, Guizhou).

going to an exorcist temple to request the mask of exorcist for a baptismal ritual. In Miao ethnic group area, it is the Chinese New Year outdoor gathering in the countryside, when young men and women in festival customs bearing embroidery totem animals and life symbols, playing music instrument (a toad shaped wind instrument), singing and dancing. Such festivity is actually a cultural extension from the ancient custom of worshipping heaven and earth at the suburb of the capital.

The Pure Brightness Festival

The Pure Brightness Festival is the time when Chinese worship nature and their ancestors. To worship ancestors is the centerpiece of the art works on the subject.

A society of natural farming economy employed slash-and-burn cultivation, burning mountains and destroying forest. Spring was a time when grass and trees start sprouting. To keep a balanced ecology and to preserve a better living environment was a necessity to human being's own survival. It was said in *Li Ji*, "During this month, the air pressure of the sky comes down and the air pressure of earth rises up. When the sky and earth come together, grass and trees germinate. It is an edict from god to start farming." "It calls to respect mountains, forests, rivers and ponds, and to preserve female animals." To alert people not to cut trees, nor to kill female livestock in the time of spring propagation, no fire was allowed on the Pure Brightness Day. All cooked food had to be made the day before. On this day, every household had willow twigs on the door to welcome the arrival of spring. People also wore willow twig in their hair, and prepared lots of steamed bread or floury flower of "Cold swallow" to put on willow branches and jujube twigs to hang from the ceiling. It was a way to mimic the spring time on earth for the return of birds and swallows. A floury flower "Swallow plate" was a symbol of the universe,

Floury flower "Cold swallow" hanging inside the cave (Yanchuan, Shaanxi).

Floury flower "Swallow plate," showing rotating border flower decoration, with a mother swallow in the center holding the light in the mouth, surrounded by a flock of young swallows (Zhongyang, Shanxi).

Red flower origami, with colorful ribbons radiating as sun rays, placed on ancestors' tombs on the Pure Brightness Day (Yan'an, Shaanxi).

The "Pure Brightness Cone" plugged on the tomb of ancestors to worship by Miao ethnic group (Chishui, Guizhou).

"Fotuo" origami of Manchurian ethnic group to place on ancestors' tomb to worship (Xinbin, Liaoning).

with a full fledged swallow and a bunch of young swallows perching on it.

In central China's northern Shaanxi area, a large paper-cut of fishnet symbol is placed over the tomb of the ancestors on the Pure Brightness Day. It was the same symbol of perpetual life from 6,000-year-old Banpo Culture. Origami in green and red paper in the shape of character "Wan," a symbol of revolving perpetuity, are scattered around the tomb. In northeast China, Manchurian makes a 3-segment "sky reaching" post to place on ancestor's tomb, with a large white flower (the sun) on the top and colorful ribbon pendants as the "sun rays."

For Miao ethnic group in the southwest region, it is the "Pure Brightness Cone" for their ancestors. A single cone is for parents; two for grandparents; and three for ancestors from great grandparents and up. A bamboo pole goes through the cone with every layer reaching out to the sky. There are three segments above the top layer, carrying three branches and three flowers on each segment pointing in different directions, a total of nine branches and nine flowers. On the very top is a large white flower with colorful ribbon pendants to carry money. The Pure Brightness Cone symbolizes the origin of life, and the branches and flowers are the tree of life.

The Dragon Boat Festival

The dragon boat festival is a totem festival. Falling on the 5th of the fifth lunar month, it is close to the summer solstice. Pestilence, as a result of the heat and dampness, is at its worst, threatening lives of human community. Images of legendary animals and totem animals are pasted on the door or carried along for safeguard. Inevitably, the theme of art works for this festival is awareness of life and safety.

Chinese mugwort was considered a magic herbal medicine to cure heat and damp related disease in ancient time. As a result, mugwort became a

Folk paper-cut the "Eight diagrams gourd" to keep evil spirits away on the Dragon Boat Day during the fifth lunar month (Jiaocheng, Shanxi).

Mugworth hanging on the door of every household on the Dragon Boat Day (Songtao, Guizhou).

Talisman bags that mothers have kids wear on the Dragon Boat Day (Zhengning, Gansu).

legendary panacea to idol. According to the Chinese local chronicles, "Use cattail on the Dragon Boat Day and insert mugwort at the door side prevent bad luck and get rid of illness", and "paste cattail and mugwort paper cow on the door on The Dragon Boat Day keeps sickness away." In the fifth lunar month, every household started hanging red ornaments, putting out cattail dragon or mugwort tiger, and decorating windows with auspicious red paper toad. Young girls cut out character "Fu" in layers for good luck; and small kids wore bright red toad made of broomcorn, garlic, and other plants to ease the heat of the summer and keep off disease. These customs are still widely practiced today as folk festivities on the Dragon Boat Day.

The Dragon Boat Festival for the people in northern Guizhou was to make totem dog with mugwort and hang it on lintels. It would be kept there till the following year, and then added more mugwort to it. It grew bigger every year to over 2 meters long. Both Han and Miao nationalities followed the same custom. If a kid got sick, they would take some mugwort from the dog's tail and boiled it in water as medicine, which would rid of pestilence. Shaanxi, a tiger totem area, people hanged mugwort tiger on the lintel. Nowadays, it has changed to using stuffed

Vest with "Five poisonous" symbols to keep the evil spirits away (Qianyang, Shaanxi).

"mugwort tiger" made in fabric and stuffed with dried mugwort incense. Stuffed tiger is sewed on children's clothes on the Dragon Boat Day for safeguard. Its lovely puffy shape gained the name of "Ai tiger," Some kids wear a stuffed tiger and a rooster on each shoulder as a local saying goes: "The rooster holds you in the mouth, and the cat (tiger) watches over you."

From eastern Gansu to Central Shaanxi plains, people wear vests with totem frog and tiger symbols as antidotes to the five poisonous (snake, scorpion, lizard, beetle and centipede). Kids carry on their backs stuffed mugwort animals like snake, frog, crab (its eight feet symbolize the sun rays), with "five poisonous" pendants. On the chest are small ornaments of legendary animal figures stuffed with dried mugwort, including the snake, the monkey, the rat, the dragon, the horse, the cow or plant bags of the pumpkin, the garlic, the grape, the peach, and the bean. There are also symbols of perpetual life like the eight diagrams lenses, star anise, or broomcorn, pyramid-shaped

Talisman ornaments as antidotes to the five poisonous creatures.
1. Tiger ornament (Qingyang, Gansu)
2. Garlic ornament (Zhengning, Gansu)
3. Gourd ornament (Qingyang, Gansu)
4. Mugworth stuffed tiger (Zhengning, Gansu)
5. Eight diagrams ornament (Qingyang, Gansu)

spider

lizard

beetle

snake/frog

eight diagrams lenses

crab

"Five poisonous" ornaments in the shape of spider, lizard, snake/frog and beetle, crab and eight diagrams lenses dumpling (Zhengning, Gansu)

dumplings, lotus bud fireworks, book casket, fan, etc., a variety collection. Their creative, casual design seemed far better than the embroidery craft works with complicated design and intensive craftsmanship.

In Yanmen Pass area, northern Shanxi, the symbol of perpetuity must be pasted in the center of the lintel on the Dragon Boat Day. There are two types, the "Haystack" and the "Silver ingot," pasted above the door in the center of the lintel to keep away the "perverse trend." People also wear on them imitation articles of silver ingot; for children age 3 and younger on the shoulder; and age five or older on the back. Girls put it in their hair braids.

"Haystack" (Daixian County, Shanxi).

"Silver ingot" (Daixian County, Shanxi).

Another custom is to eat *zongzi* pyramid-shaped steamed dumplings made with glutinous rice, red bean and jujubes wrapped in reed leaves. Imitation of its hexagon shape or square is one of the most popular ornaments to wear on the occasion. With blue, red, white, yellow and black threads winding around it, it is quite eyes-catching. The colors of the threads stand for spring (blue), summer (red), long summer (white), fall (yellow), and winter (black). These are the colors of grass and trees from sprouting to withering a year round. In the eyes of the Chinese community, red, yellow, blue, white and black five colors are

Pyramid-shaped dumpling ornament (Zhengning, Gansu).

the colors that compose the universe.

In folk paper-cut and embroidery works, animals holding grass in the mouth are legendary animals, not natural animals, such as a "Fish holding grass in the mouth," or a rooster, a deer, a rabbit, a sheep, a tiger, a snake, etc. The animals with acrimony appeared in some local art works are connected with the primitive totem symbols idolized in that area. Mugwort was later sanctified by Taoism as "glossy ganoderma." Then the grass accompanying the totem animals also changed to "A deer holding glossy ganoderma in the mouth," or a tiger, a snake "holding glossy ganoderma in the mouth." These animals were considered symbol of good fortune and celestial being. However, the original art form of "A snake holding mugwort in the mouth" was from the 5,000-year-old painted pottery unearthed from Xiangfen of Shanxi Province. The grass in that painting should be mugwort. The same is true in the paper-cut "A snake twining round a rabbit" and "A snake holding grass in the mouth," which are still quite popular in this area today.

Dragon has been a totem figure for all nationalities in China. The 5th of the fifth lunar month is the Dragon Boat Day. Every year on this day, the bustling dragon boat race along the Yangtze River valley; and nationwide festivities like the dragon lantern fair, dragon dance, lion (belong to tiger branch) dance, are of great cultural and art values.

Mid-Autumn Festival moon cake pattern showing the "Sal tree of life" and the jade hare from the moon palace (Jishan, Shanxi).

The Mid-Autumn Festival

Chinese folk custom believes that spring is the time to worship and fall to pay back. Spring worship welcomes all saints from heaven and earth, mainly god of the sun; and fall payback is to pay tribute to the generous, load carrying mother earth at the end of a harvest year. To offer respect to the land, the moon, and mother's body is a humane culture extended from matriarchal society. Eating moon cake is a palatable custom of the Mid-Autumn Festival. The moon cake relief patterns are numerous and colorful, both in terms of art and cultural implication. Fairy tales told through moon cake relief patterns include "A pairing fish;" "Baby with coiled hair;" "Sal tree of life;" and story of the jade hare from the moon palace.

Folk customs of moon worship vary from region to region in China. The most unforgettable I have seen was in central Shanxi. An altar was set up in the

Worship the moon at the Mid-Autumn Festival (Daixian County, Shanxi).

yard to burn incense and candles. Layers of fruits piled up on the altar as offerings to the moon fairy. Placed in the middle of the altar was a huge round cake of one-meter in diameter, showing patterns of radiating lotus pedals coming from the center and colorful floury flowers and figures like "Monkey eating a peach." In between of the lotus pedals were jujubes, symbolic of life and propagation. The cake, likening lotus to the moon and

Floury flower to worship the moon at Mid-Autumn Festival. Photo by Qiao Xiaoguang.

mother's body, was a prayer for a bumper harvest, family reunion and prosperity.

From the ancient folk fables and unearthed articles, the sun is always connected with a golden crow or a legendary Fusang tree; while the moon is linked to the moon toad, the jade hare and the laurel. The sun and the moon always move around the sky, rising from the east and setting to the west. It reflects human's basic knowledge of life and its perpetuity. The moon toad and the medicine mortar are female symbols in the family of the universe. The rabbit is god of proliferation; and the Fusang, the laurel and the Sal are the tree of life. Together, those symbols and images made up a fairy tale that has been told and passed down for thousands of years. Obviously, moon worship is the main theme of folk art works on the Mid-Autumn Festival.

China is a multi-ethnic nation. Each nationality and every geographical region has its own custom festivities. Miao ethnic group worships ancestors by thumping cows; Yi and Bai ethnic groups have the Torch Festival; others like the "Pan King's day" of Yao ethnic group, Tibetan New Year (lunar calendar used by Tibetan ethnic group), Oboo Festival in Inner Mongolia, and Paiwan ethnic group's celebration of harvest in Taiwan, etc. It is through this array of festivals that folk art is seeded, grown and blossomed.

Folk Arts in Daily Life

Residential Building

Chinese residential architecture also embodies original Chinese philosophy. The basic style for residential architecture in China is: horizontally following the five elements (metal, wood, water, fire, and earth) and the eight diagrams; vertically exhibiting sky-reaching and *yin-yang* matching. Whether it is a cave or a house; it is of wood or brick structure; rammed earth construction or bamboo construction; it is all regarded as the entire entity of the universe. Living in it is to live in mother's body of the universe. The same is true with residential building decorations.

Horizontal style architecture—The five elements and the eight diagrams. In northern China, houses are built in courtyard style, or quadrangle; and in southern China, houses feature "Bamboo structure with a skylight in the center." Both styles embody the philosophy that the universe consists of four sides and five elements around one center. The same layout of square bricks in a rotating pattern is seen on the screen wall in the quadrangle courtyard in Beijing; as well as in the three-room and a

Pottery miniature courtyard among the burials during the Three Kingdoms Period (220–280) unearthed from Echeng, Hubei, showing ancient Chinese residential building in a five elements and eight diagrams style.

screen wall style house in Yunnan.

Vertical style architecture— The vertical pillar in Chinese traditional wood structure building is a sky-reaching symbol that connects heaven and earth. Its base is earth, in the form of a stone drum or a golden melon symbolizing mother's body—the origin of life, and the top crossbeam is the sky.

Residential building featuring four quarters with a center skylight to represent the five element universal view in Kunming, Yunnan.

The *yin-yang* view in house building is shown in two *yin-yang* pillars heading down towards earth and crossing tails at the "sky beam." It is the same concept as the view on dragon totem that *yin-yang* dragons having their heads on earth and mating in heaven. The closure of the building is the connecting point of two dragons. A rite of worship is held on the closing day and an eight diagrams graphic is pasted over the closing point. A pair of crossing chopsticks is placed on top, forming a symbol of perpetual life, with a black cloth rooster in the center as the symbol of the sun.

Residential building decoration—In northern China where people idolize fish and dragon, the two pillars in residential house are made in the form of *yin-yang* dragons with heads down and tails up crossed at the sky beam. In southern China, they are in the form of two phoenixes, and in Yunnan among Yi and Bai ethnic groups, they are *yin-yang* tigers. Dai ethnic group who idolizes peacock and elephant, the two pillars are in the form of peacocks. A decorative symbol in the center of the sky beam as the "central flower" is a universal cultural code of Chinese architecture.

The "central flower" is made in a variety of forms. In the Yangtze River valley, it is a four-pedal evergreen flower made with four inverted tiles, a prototype of bamboo style architecture from Hemudu Culture. The "central flower" in Anhui, Jiangxi, Hunan, Sichuan, Guizhou, and Yunnan are made with three titles shaped into a Chinese word "pin," known as "three letter stack," or "three hats." It is believed that such symbol keeps away the evil spirits and provides safety at all seasons. There is also "coin flower" or "gourd flower." Yi and Bai ethnic groups in Yunnan Province are black or white tiger totem lovers. Their symbol on the sky beam center is a tile cat.

Recently people found that in Anhui Province, a plane view of a boat-shaped housing complex was a symbol for character "Gui," symbolic of family prosperity. "Gui" is a vertical philosophy symbol as reaching the sky. It is very rare to use a vertical symbol in place of a horizontal symbol in Chinese residential architecture.

From the north to the south, Chinese wood carving window frame for residential house vary a great deal. However, its theme remains the same at all time. In Zhejiang, Fujian, Jiangxi, Anhui and northern

A side view of Chinese residential house with a cultural symbol of *yin-yang* mating to reach the sky (Dengfeng, Henan).

Shanxi, folk artists created a variety of decorative animal figures and folk stories in wood carving window frames, with superb craftsmanship, which, coupled with a wide range of brick carving and stone carving art works, forms a complete folk fine art series in residential architecture.

On the Loess Plateau of northern China, cave is the residential house for the local people. The vault of the cave is considered the sky, and the floor is earth. To live under the round sky and on square earth is to live inside mother's body of the universe. The facade is the wood structure portion with an arched door and window. Above the middle cross bar is considered the sky,

An architecture symbol of two mating *yin-yang* peacocks on a Dai ethnic group building in Xishuangbanna, Yunnan. Dai national idolizes peacock totem.

A building of Yunnan Bai ethnic group, a tiger totem worshiper, showing a pair of *yin-yang* tiger with tails crossing at the sky beam.

Diamond shaped paper-cut "thirty-six lattice window of clouds."

and the middle lattice is a sky window, with slanting lattices on the left and the right. Below the cross bar is the 36 lattice as a symbol of the universe. At Chinese New Year, a large paper-cut of a red "rotating flower" is pasted in the center of the sky window; and a totem animal in the middle of the 36 lattice, with four corner flowers, making a diamond square "36 lattice windows of clouds." This is a theme art work featuring perpetual life in residential architecture. The cave door is also fully decorated. The threshold is earth, and the cross bar lintel is the sky. Two raised carving objects in round, rotating pattern on the cross bar are symbols of the sun and the moon. There are two animal stone blocks sitting at each side of the door. At times, it is hard to select a perfect geographical

A residential cave on the Loess Plateau (Suide, Shaanxi).

spot and the cave is built with a view of uneven mountain passes from afar. As this was considered a vicious sign by the locals, the owner of the cave would need to forge a stone cylinder to set up in front of the cave door for safeguard. However, this safeguard device was later used to tie up donkeys or horses, and became known mistakenly as the "horse stake." The stone cylinder is often decorated with auspicious patterns like "Eight men bringing in treasures," "Monkeys eating peaches."

With its simple, unpretentious style and a variety of designs, it has become known as the horse stake art series.

In northern Shaanxi, it is customary to paste various symbols on top of a newly erected cave for safeguard. These symbols, rooted in original Chinese philosophy, rep-

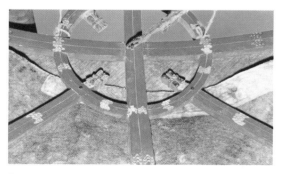

Symbol of radiating sun rays on the vault of a yurt (Baotou, Inner Mongolia).

resent an important part in folk art.

Cuisine

The culture of Chinese cuisine also embodies original Chinese philosophy concept. The art form that represents this culture comes in two folds, geometry form and form of nature, which mainly consists of animal figures.

Geometry symbols: In social rituals, the all-time theme is where human life comes from. It is mother's body of the universe that breeds all living things on earth. What does it look like? Chinese believed that it was like the shape of steamed bread with a round sky (and flat earth) and red beans inside. Therefore, they made

Chinese New Year meal—eating dumplings, Wonton and grain twister on the first of the lunar year.

Wonton and grain twister.

Big "Guo Kui," a special food product of Shandong, with a facial pattern as a symbol of the rotating sun.

"Wonton" to celebrate birth. The theme on wedding ceremony is to produce life through matching male and female, yin and yang. Therefore, the gift bread is "cereal twist," a geometry code imitating inter-winding of *yin-yang*, with jujubes in between as

Floury flower—Jujubes Mountain, for Chinese New Year (Zhongyang, Shanxi).

The process of making floury flower.

symbol of life. When life ends, it goes back to the "wonton" universe, then there would be no more red bean in the steamed bread. However, a red dot or a rotating code is painted on the top to symbolize the sun. In custom festivals, when the land warms up to start spring, traditional food for Chinese is "jiaozi"(dumpling) and "hezi," homonym for making kids.

The other art form is the totem animal symbol displayed in Chinese food and eating culture. In areas where fish and frog are idolized, people believe that life come from mother's body of *yin-yang* fish or *yin-yang* frog. Therefore, they make holiday bread in the shape of

A housewife making a birthday gift bread of a pair of *yin-yang* sheep (Cixian County, Hebei).

a pair of fish; or a pair of tigers in areas of tiger idol; or a tiger head on a dragon body with fish tail; implying integration of earth and the sky. For sheep-idol area, it is a pair of sheep, or three sheep that marks a new beginning.

The floury flower made into geometry or animal symbols are deemed as patron saint, and saint of propagation. Therefore, they are supposed to be made for family or relatives only in order to benefit the family. On the day of Sheep Festival in Hebei, people make floury sheep and eat it too. As a folk proverb goes, "you have the head and I have the foot, we all live till ninety-nine years old." Eating floury sheep is believed to help keep the family safe and maintain longevity.

On Chinese New Year, floury flowers are served for various reasons, from a wish for health and longevity for family members and loves ones; to a prayer for a harvest year and good fortune. At the start of spring ploughing, people bury certain food underground for god of earth praying for a bumper harvest. On the Pure

Gift bread for the worship of ancestors (Anyang, Gansu).

Brightness Day, floury flower is to worship ancestors and ask for blessings of their spirits in heaven. Floury flower with these implications are meant to be consumed, therefore, they are rarely painted.

In few places, floury flower are painted in colors like the "cold swallow" for the Pure Brightness Festival in Daixian County, Shanxi; and the floury flower in Guanxian County, Shandong. These are made for offerings, not for consumption,

Some cuisine art works are made for large-scale annual worship of ancestors, god, past emperors and warriors. The ceremonial bread for such occasions is usually made with exquisite style and bright colors. An example in this category is the butter flower from Tibetan ethnic group, a variety of vivid human figures, animals, plants and religious events made with solid butter, delicately carved and beautifully painted. They are often displayed at Tibetan and Buddhist worship services in Potala Palace in Tibet, Kumbum Monastery in Qinghai, Labrang Monastery in Gansu, Meidaizhao Monastery in Inner Mongolia, and Yonghe Lama Temple in Beijing.

Holiday bread "swallow platter" is a round three-layer sandwich filled with jujubes on each layer (some with eggs and jujubes). According to local folks, "it is Chinese New Year bread. In spring, swallows are coming back, and the 'swallow platter' is to make a nest for them." The three layers symbolize the sky, people and earth; and the jujubes and eggs are meant for good harvest and lots of children.

In northern Shaanxi, a floury flower used as tribute to god on Chinese New Year is the "mountain of jujubes," made with winding noodles and jujubes in between in a pattern of "a snake twining round eggs." The jujube is a symbol of good harvest and many children. In Shanxi, the "mountain of jujubes" is "Two babies (a boy and a girl) with coiled hair," representing Fuxi and Nüwa, two very first ancestors of Chinese nationals according to an ancient fairy tale.

Dress and Adornment

Embroidery art in dress and adornment also embodies original Chinese philosophy. Likening human body to the universe, the upper part (the head) is the sky, the lower part (the feet) is the earth, and the middle (the pubic area) is the center. The understanding of this leads to the culture implication of Chinese dress and adornment.

Many folk dress and adornment are designed as philosophy symbols. It is a custom for women in northern Shaanxi to wear a pleated apron girdle when cooking on the second day after getting married. It is meant to show off the embroidery work on the waistband, usually patterns of two *yin-yang* tiger heads; pig heads, or fish heads connected at the waist. In eastern Gansu plains,

Paper-cut as embroidery patterns for making Miao ethnic group's costume: a national heroine (Taijiang, Guizhou).

Silver crown with the totem of sun and ox horns worn by Miao women in Guizhou.

Birds-eye view of Gelao ethnic group's pleated skirt and a tassel cap in the center as a symbol of the sun (Jieping, Guizhou).

central Shaanxi plains and southern Shanxi plains, the Han Nationality idolizes tiger totem, therefore, people would wear vests with a tiger symbol to conquer the five poisonous insects; or wearing a tiger hat, a pair of tiger shoes and a tiger undergarment. On the bed, it is tiger pillows, blankets, dye-printed or wax-printed tiger cloth wrappers; and on the door screen is "a tiger coming down the mountain. " This is nothing short of being a family member of the tiger clan.

Among the costumes of Yi ethnic group in Huangping, Guizhou, a headwear named tassel hat, is a round hat in the shape of the sun with radiating tassels like the sun rays and an arrow on top aiming at the sun. Looking down from the middle of the tassel hat as the pleated skirt opens up; it is a visual symbol of the sun radiating from the center. Yi women describe it as this, "their hat symbolizes the sun carrying an arrow in the center. In ancient times, there were total of 13 suns and 13 moons up in the sky. Unbearable to live under that condition, the ancestors of Yi shot down 12 suns and 12 moons with silver arrows, leaving only one of each." The costume and the headwear today are part of that legend.

In the Miao villages in southeastern Guizhou, women wear a silver crown to idolize the sun and ox totem. The decorative silvery brightly glitters from the center of sun between the ox horns. A matching pleated skirt is from waist down, symbolizing sun rays. Miao embroidery boasts a variety of categories, besides flat embroidery; there are also tied embroidery, plated embroidery, crape embroidery, and others. Flat embroidery is often used for sleeves; double layer embroidery for collar flower; and weaving embroidery on waist bands. It is worth mentioning that each branch of Miao ethnic group has its own costume as national identity which can not be changed. Even the direction of the needle goes when embroidering is set in certain ways. On the lower part of the pleated skirt are three horizontal thread lines which tell another story. In remote antiquity, a large scale war was waged between the army from the emperor and Chiyou, ancestor of Miao ethnic group, which ended in Chiyou's defeat. To have later generations always re-member the

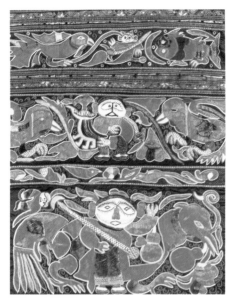

Miao ethnic group's embroidery dress for women, "Ancient songs of Miao ethnic group" (Kaili, Guizhou).

hardship that their ancestors went through, they embroider three lines on the skirt to exhibit the route that their ancestor took to migrate south after the war. From the top down, the first line was to cross the Yellow River; then the Yangtze River; finally the Yuan River before settling down at the Miao villages in Guizhou. Another unique costume is the "hundred birds"

Birds-eye view of a pleated skirt (Miao ethnic group) as a symbol of the sun (Guizhou).

Wax batiking work of Bai ethnic group (Dali, Yunnan).

Women's dress and adornment of Yi ethnic group (Ningliang, Yunnan).

blouse, an embroidery dragon with a bird head against the green bottom to tell a Miao ethnic group fairy tale. Without any crop seeds at first, the Miao family had been eating tree leaves for food until bird Ji Yu carried their ancestor up to heaven to be granted crop seeds by god. Using a variety of styles in embroidery and drawing from resourceful art images based on legends and fairy tales recorded in the "Ancient songs of Miao ethnic group," women in the Miao villages have created exquisite embroidery art on their costumes and clothes with ultimate delicacy. It is a master piece of Chinese embroidery art.

Yi ethnic group in southwest China idolizes black tiger totem. Black, regarded as the color of the sun, is the color of their national costume. Women dress in black skirts, and men in slacks wearing a black turban with a symbol in the middle pointing to the sky. It is a symbol of absolute sacredness referred to as the "Buddha of heaven." There are also symbols in the shape of a character "Ren" meaning people, or a rotating tie towards the sky. Women's headwear is a square cap with a rotating cross in the center. The embroidery symbols on their clothes or tobacco bags bear distinct masculine spirit. Examples like a radiating diagram symboling "The autumn moon;" "Red sickle flower;" are some of the representative works. Yi ethnic group's costume share similar design and pattern with the designs on Majiayao antiques unearthed in the northwest regions. It is reasonable to say that, Yi's ancestors, who migrated from the northwest to the southwest in ancient times, were the creators of Majiayao Culture.

Bai ethnic group worships white tiger, therefore, white is the main color of their national costume and headwear. Butterfly, octagonal petal flower and octagonal diagram are favorite subjects of their embroidery works to idolize the sun.

Likewise, from the attire of Naxi ethnic group who idolizes sheep totem, a northwestern tribal culture featuring farming and animal

Women's dress and adornment of Naxi ethnic group (Lijiang, Yunnan).

Costume and ornament of Bai ethnic group.

husbandry can be traced. Naxi women's headwear is a roll of blue cloth in a half circle, matched with a stripe cross on the chest and white sheep leather skirt laced with black sheep hair.

In Dawu Mountain in Taiwan, the attire of the Paiwan and Rukai ethnic groups reflect a culture of "the hundred-step snake" totem. It was said that the ancestor of Paiwan ethnic group was direct descendant of the sun. The sun placed an egg in a jar, which was earth, to be incubated by a male and a female snake, and that started children of Paiwan ethnic group. Paiwan national costume is the dress code at annual harvest worship and wedding ceremonies. Symbols of "the hundred-step snake" totem are embroidered on their clothes and hats. From the front, we see two snakes on the shoulders and sleeves; two more on the pants one on each leg. From the back, the top part is their humanized ancestor, flanked by two *yin-yang* snakes that bred him; the lower part is like the tail of a wild boar, symbolizing sun rays. The cap has a sun glass in the middle, surrounded by a circle of "hundred-step snake" symbols. For seniors, the sun glass is decorated with wild boar teeth. Women wear snake necklace; and men wear "hero belt" with symbols of "hundred-step snake." Against a black background, the sketches of glittering golden snake from the head to the feet are very glamorous. On special occasions, all invited guests, even the outsiders, are expected to be in Paiwan national dress.

In Yanbian, Jilin Province, it is customary to have one-year-old baby wear embroidery waistband made by the mother or the grandmother which bears over 60 different types of embroidery decorative symbols, including humanized tiger, eight diagrams sun flower; embroidery ball, triangle, egg plant, garlic, etc. It is a wish for the baby to live over 60 years in age.

With Manchurian wedding custom, male needs to wear a headgear when he gets married. It is sewed with 8 pieces of black cloth into a circular cone shape pointing to the sky, with a red sun symbol on top. Women's headwear is a triangle-shaped sun flower. In the Qing Dynasty, male Manchuria's "fall hat"(warm hat) and "summer hat" (cool hat) were all white and shaped in circular cone,

Men's festival costume of Paiwan ethnic group for the occasion of celebrating harvest (Dawu Mountain, Taiwan)

topped by a ball as the sun carrying radiating red straps as sun rays. Female hat was called "Qitou," a symbol of swallow tail wing developed from the art design "double coiled hair." Manchurians also embroider lotus on shoe soles as they put it "stepping on lotus flower will convert into a Buddha," meaning to become immortal.

Xinjiang Uygur ethnic group's headwear is made with 4 pieces of cloth, with embroidery patterns of the tree of life, the flower of life or *badam* apricot seeds from the tree of life. Their "sky-reaching" headwear and striped shirts and pants have become a unique cultural symbol with distinct national characteristics.

Travel

The theme of transportation is to "travel safe." Art works for decoration on vehicles and horses are mostly symbols of "good luck" or an "eight diagrams." At Maojin ferry, Henan, on the midstream of the Yellow River, an area where monkey totem is idolized, a decorative monkey totem is placed on the mast tip of all boats that sail in the Yellow River. A line underneath reads: "The general is a trailblazer; and the lieutenant general is strong and invincible. " The monkey totem is there to protect everyone on board when sailing amidst high winds and waves in the Yellow River.

Folk Arts in Beliefs and Taboos

Human lives were often threatened by irresistible natural or man-made vicious power. At the time when a society was scientifically undeveloped, humans were even more confined in their understanding of the universe. As a result, people believed that there was an invisible world of ghosts, evil spirits, demons and monsters that could harm human life; on the other hand, they also believed that there was a supernatural power that could help conquer the evil and protect their existence. China's unique history and cultural background over several thousand years since primitive society helped sustain the influence of totem and fairy idols, which also has an impact on folk art works.

The Worship of God

Women from the Loess Plateau created a wide range of sophisticated paper-cut series featuring patron-saint and propagation-saint, "Baby with coiled hair." When there was flood from continuous pouring rain, they had paper-cut "Sweeping wife" or "Sweeping mother" holding broom in one hand and a dust pin in the other to sweep away the clouds; during a time of drought, "Baby with coiled hair" was pasted with head down on the water vat to pray for rain; in case of sickness, "Spirit calling baby;" "Fairies from five paths," and "Sun flower seeds doll" in yellow paper were pasted on the lintel to drive away ghosts and vicious spirits. To pray for more children at wedding was to put out paper-cuts "Happy baby;" "Lotus flower baby;" and "Pomegranate baby," etc.

In Northeast area, propagation-saint in folk art works bear designated functional characteristics. Manchuria's "Wet-nurse saint" takes care of marriage of the sons in the family; "Tiger nurse saint" leads the way in mountain roads; Heilongjiang's "Jiqiya saint" helps with disease and disasters; and "Baby holding a magic grass in hand" in Xinjiang calls back human spirit.

Totem animals or legendary animals are often characterized by the geographical regions. Pasted on the

"Fairies from five paths" (Yanchuan, shaanxi).

"A thousand piece net" for the worship of god: linking individual pieces from each household and hang it on the top of the shrine inside the temple (Qianyang, Shaanxi).

doors in yellow glossy paper are local patron-saints varying from area to area, a deer or a rooster in Inner Mongolia; a tiger or "baby with coiled hair riding a tiger" in central China; a monkey or "baby with coiled hair riding a monkey, or riding a cow," in Henan, etc.

Along the mid-stream of the Yellow River , people congregate to worship. All the women in the village participate in making a-hundred-piece, or a-thousand-piece embroidery net. Each household makes one square piece of an animal figure or a plant, and then the whole village come together and makes them into one big lucky cross to hang on the top of the temple.

Household Objects

Daily-use appliance, besides its practical function, is interpreted as a symbol in folk custom and folk art.

Umbrella—its shape reminds people of the sun. When I was in Miao villages in Guizhou, one day I came back home in the rain holding an umbrella, my host said to me in a serious tone to fold the umbrella away and place it behind the door so nobody could touch it. People's belief in umbrella later turned into making it a classy symbol as "canopy" and "yellow gauze umbrella." It was used exclusively in the temple over the statues of saint, or by the imperial family for shade outdoors.

Five-elements and eight diagrams Paper-cut "Awl and scissors keep the house out of the harm's way" (Houma, Shanxi).

Fan—fan was at one time a favorable idol in China. Later, it was introduced to Japan where the sun was the ultimate image and received even higher and more sacred worship. The shape of an unfolding fan fits the visual image of the rising sun from the horizon, fanning out sun rays, just like the morning sun rising from the eastern sky.

Scissors—Scissors idol in folk art works is a nation-wide custom. According to an old saying, "An awl and a pair of scissors keep the house out of the harm's way." Scissors have always been regarded an item for safeguard. Paper-cut "Eight pairs of scissors pointing to the center to form a ball flower;" and "A pair of scissors pointing upward with a scorpion on top;" are popular patterns seen on the door for safeguard at the Dragon Boat Festival.

Ax—Ax is another image in folk art works. It was first seen on painted pottery of 6,000-year-old Yangshao Culture from Miaodigou, Linru, Henan, and pottery carving of Dawenkou Culture in Shandong. Then the same image was found on the pottery from the primitive-society cultural relics in Shijiahe, Hubei. It is believed that along the Yangtze River valley to the Yellow River basin, ax had been a symbol to safeguard house and tomb from evil spirits and epidemics for several thousand years, and it is still being used today.

Abstract Symbols

The image of *yin-yang* fairy and gourd in the shape of half fish, half bird can be traced back to 6,000-year-old Yangshao Culture. According to the fairy tale about the beginning of human life, in ancient time, when flood surging to the sky, Fuxi and his sister Nüwa stayed in a gourd to keep from getting drowned. By that, gourd has always been a symbol of mother's body which created all things on earth. In Miao villages, this symbol is a gourd flute; in northern China, it is in the form of paper-cut and embroidery works like "Eight diagrams gourd;" "Double nozzle gourd;" "Gourd laying kids;" and "Gourd over a square;" and a variety of gourd shaped hand bags. When pasted on the bridal chamber, it is considered a happy symbol for propagation; on the door front, it keeps away vicious spirits and

Chinese Folk custom to worship rising cones, "Three cones reach out to the sky" (Jianchuan, Yunnan).

epidemics; wearing on the chest, it is patron-saint, and in residential building, gourd is usually being placed on the sky beam of the central room for safeguard.

From primitive society to present, some commonly accepted symbols of life also have functional characteristics in social beliefs and taboos. A dot is usually a symbol of god. To wear on the chest, it is a symbol of patron-saint; to draw a dot on an animal figure, the animal becomes a supernature symbol. I saw such a dot on a pottery pig unearthed from 7,000-year-old Hemudu Cultural relics. It should be a legendary pig which was in the category of the sun animals. On the rock carving in Lascaux, France, dated back 15,000 years ago, the leg-

Paper-cut—eight diagrams gourd (Ansai, Shaanxi).

endary ox was also labeled with a dot. Obviously, it had been a recognized philosophical and cultural code for the entire mankind and had been around for some 15,000 years.

"Good fortune," "Eight diagrams," and "Snake twining round nine eggs" are symbols for safe travel often seen on vehicles, horse saddle and gear, boats and ships. They are also used for residential houses and buildings. These symbols are on each side of the entrance to the tent in Tibet or yurt in Mongolia. The in-house symbol of Tibetan dwelling, a constitution of mountains, the moon and the sun, is of the same nature and function. It was first seen on house-ware carvings from Dawenkou Culture in Shandong Province.

"China net" hanging along both sides of the street during "SARS" epidemic in 2003 (Beijing).

The Structure of Chinese Folk Art

Chinese folk art is vastly different from Western traditional art in philosophy concept, art structure and form, and color composition.

Philosophy Concept

Chinese folk art and the art of Chinese officialdom and professional artists share the same philosophy base. They are rooted in the same comprehension that heaven and human, objects and subjects are of one entity; and they are based on the same cosmic ontology. However, folk art is a continuation of the original Chinese philosophy, a straightforward display of this philosophy; whereas the art of the literati and officialdom only draws from its concept to express personal feelings of the artists.

Rural female laborers are among the main creators of Chinese folk art, especially in categories such as paper-cut. In my observation of their entire process of creative art, they were indeed expressing their understanding of the universe through art works, using a language from the original mode of philosophical symbols. That is a common nature of all communal art. The individuality of their art work lies in the variance of the symbols and codes related with their national identity and geographical region; their emotional temperament and the cultural attainment of the creator, and the art form and language they choose. Folk art is a kind of personalized art. The common nature of folk art is displayed through individual art works.

Take fish for example, according to ancient Greek philosophy, which is the base of Western philosophy, "art is a mirror image of nature;"(Heraclitus) "artist's skill depicting visual objects."

A painting of motionless carp by 19th-century French impressionist artist Edward Marne.

Chinese artist Li Kuchan's work expressing personal emotion from the story "Joy on the water bank to reveal the true feeling in the love world, and pursue the romantic idea" recorded in "The Autumn Water" of *Zhuang Zi*.

(Aristotle) Under that theory, the goal of an artist is to copy the objective natural world, and the best lifelike imitation would be the ultimate achievement in art. Therefore, the art is about studying the structure and the color pattern of natural objects; judging their physical existence in terms of quality, quantity and space. To draw a fish for the best imitation, it would have to pull the fish out of the water and place it in a basket in order to convey that feel of quality, quantity and space, even the smell. This is what they call a "motionless object." This theory of creative art is determined by the philosophy that fish and human are two separate entities, and the nature and the society are opposite worlds. This actually has been the philosophical and aesthetical base of western art for over 2,000 years.

On the other hand, Chinese philosophy and art structure is the unity of nature and human and integration of objects and ego (subjects). To Chinese artists, I am the fish and the fish is me. If I paint a fish swimming care-free in the water, it is a way to express my own care-free state of mind. This was the same philosophy invoked by the Chinese philosopher Zhuang Zi in "The Autumn Water" of *Zhuang Zi*. Looking at fish by a pond with a friend, Zhuang Zi said to his friend, "The fish swimming in the water are so happy." The friend replied, "Not a fish yourself, how would you know?" "Not being me, how do you know that I don't

Folk paper-cut "Eight diagrams fish" implying *yin-yang* view and perpetual life.

know?" claimed Zhuang Zi. The philosophy based on Confucian and Taoist theory to speak one's mind and convey one's emotion through an object, is the philosophical and aesthetical base of Chinese traditional art, and a technique in freehand art work. Different from the theory of Western art, Chinese paintings are generally focused on bringing out the theme of the objects regardless of being a realistic painting or a freehand brushwork.

In the eyes of folk art creators, fish is a cultural symbol that produces life through mating of *yin-yang* fish. In art form, it appears in pairs. Propagation is to continue life from generation to generation till eternity, which happens in a revolving pattern. Therefore, the art form is "Two spinning fish." The "Eight diagrams fish," with two fish on a plate towards opposite directions, implies that mother's body of the universe (the plate) contains *yin-yang* air. The interaction of the two produces life, and, through propagation, life goes on for

Porcelain buckled bowl from Luzhou, Sichuan.

ever. The "Buckled bowl," a bowl bottom upward, is a philosophy symbol. The upper lid symbolizes the sky, and the lower dish is earth, representing the blurry mother's body of the universe before the separation of earth from heaven; *yin* from *yang*. One can be separated into two, and two combined in one. In some art works, the lid opens up with a fish coming out, an implication of life being produced through unification of *yin-yang*.

The Shaping Structure

Yin-yang Structure

On Chinese New Year of the year of rat, a woman farmer named Li Aiping sent me a paper-cut of "rat coming out of a Buckled bowl," named "Rat biting open the sky." According to the folklore, rat and fish are proliferation saints. The buckled bowl symbolizes the undivided universe. On the year of rat, the rat came out to bite open the sky and started life on earth. Polyspermic plants like gourd, pumpkin, grape, are also symbols of propagation. In art works, their function of producing seeds is what it matters. Therefore, in spite that the seeds can not be seen from the outside, they are still being drawn. Once I mentioned to the women that the pumpkin seeds

Folk paper-cut "Rat biting open the sky" (Lüliang, Shanxi).

Folk paper-cut displaying the scene when the sky and earth open up, fish, the creator of the universe, comes out to produce human and all living things on earth (Huangling, Shaanxi).

Folk paper-cut "Rat eating grape" (Luochuan, Shaanxi).

were not visible, they said, "But pumpkin has seeds." Then I realized that it was not the gourd, the pumpkin or the grape that they wanted to draw, it was the seeds inside. The seeds were metaphorical of the children that were conceived by the uterus (In the form of a gourd, a pumpkin and grape) of mother's body. Original Chinese philosophy defines the basic characteristics of Chinese folk art. Likewise, "Rat eating pumpkin" and "Rat eating grape" are of the same implication.

Fish with lotus is another cultural symbol indicating the unity of earth and the sky, male and female. "Fish playing around lotus" and "Fish biting lotus" are favorite paper-cuts for Chinese New Year and wedding ceremonies. It is known to all in China that fish stands for male and the polyspermic lotus for female, but few knew the difference between "Fish playing around lotus" and "Fish biting lotus." One Chinese New Year when I was in Wuli town, Yijun of northern Shaanxi, some young girls were there making paper-cut for window decorations. I asked a girl what she was making. "Fish playing around lotus," she replied. I asked another girl, the answer was "Fish biting lotus." When asked what "fish playing lotus" meant, they smiled and said, "They are dating." "How about 'Fish biting lotus'?" Nobody responded and everybody flushed. A stand-by woman holding a baby in her arm spoke for them, "Well, they slept together." The group burst into laughter. "Fish playing around lotus" is fish playing above the water, meaning "dating;" but "Fish biting lotus" has the fish under the water to bite the lotus stem, which is "getting married." Different combinations of two images actually have a strict boundary line in implications. One girl even added a baby to her feature paper-cut "Fish biting lotus," which was named "lotus bearing seed." However, this addition couldn't be in "Fish playing around lotus." "It would be having kids without getting married," explained the woman holding a baby. Obviously, at each stage from dating, getting married to having kids, there is a corresponding art arrangement to convey it.

In paper-cut "Rooster holding a fish in the mouth" and "Fish with a rooster head," the rooster is a metaphor for the sky and of male nature; while the fish is for earth and female. That is their way of displaying the unity of heaven and earth, *yin* and *yang*, male and female in the language of art.

Paper-cut "Loving tiger", with 3 or 4 adorable baby tigers inside mother tiger's abdomen; or "Monkey eating cigarettes" showing cute baby monkeys inside mother monkey's abdomen; and a pair of birds with fledglings; etc., are also art forms expressing the theme

Paper-cut "Fish playing around lotus." With the fish being above the lotus, it implies dating.

Paper-cut "Fish biting lotus." When the fish bites the lotus stem, it implies getting married and having children.

Paper-cut for window decoration "Rats stealing oil" (Yichuan, Shaanxi).

of propagation through images of legendary animals.

The Five Elements Structure

Western artists tend to utilize focused perspective, and the literati employ traditional prosaic perspective. Following a style different from either, with Chinese folk art, the art form is based on the perspective of original Chinese philosophy. Paper-cut "Rat eating oil," in which the oil jar is a metaphor of mother's body, and the rat a symbol of having a lot of children. However, the jar opening is an arc and the bottom is a straight level line. "A jar needs to sit on a flat surface," explained the creator. Actually, in here the arc is likened to the sky and the bottom to earth; together it is a symbol of the universe with a round sky and a square earth. Unlike the cubism in Western modern art in which circles and squares are formed by geometry figures; Chinese folk art structure is counter perspective, which is based on the concepts of Chinese philosophy.

To draw a house, they perceive it from the five-element perspective. For example, when depicting a plane view of a house, they draw the front side, as well as the flank sides which cannot be seen from front, because, in their words, the house has its side walls. Painting a suitcase they would also paint the patterns on the side of the

Folk paper-cut from northern Shaanxi: "Rural family life."

Paper-cut "Community gathering on Chinese New Year" (Zhongyang, Shanxi).

suitcase even though they were not in sight from a straight perspective.

Folk paper-cut "Magpie nest" (Ansai, Shaanxi).

In depicting a scene of a community gathering in the central yard of a courtyard house, the plane view of the entire scene is fully unfolded without any overlapping. The house on the east, west, south and north four sides of the courtyard are all drawn in a flat, horizontal view, with bottom base towards the center; all human figures at the scene are laid down with their feet towards the center. This is an exemplary composition of five-element concept originated in original Chinese philosophy.

When showing rural family life, they present the scenes both inside and outside the house, from the house-ware to the people

Folk painting "Grazing" (Yijun, Shaanxi).

at the site. A side view of a tree and a front view of a magpie nest fully uncover the lovely baby magpies inside the nest. Such freelance drawing is like shooting with a movie camera, taking in what's happening along the way.

To draw a human profile portrait, they draw two eyes instead of one. When I mentioned that the other eye couldn't be seen, they claimed, "But human has two eyes."

In art work "Herd Grazing," a cowherd boy standing under a tree is given a composite head with a front and two side views, because "he has to look around to watch the herd, not just looking straight ahead. " The livestock also have a left and a

Folk paper-cut "Jiang Ziya's fishing" (Yijun, Shaanxi).

Jiang Ziya's fishing

Jiang Ziya was an outstanding militarist and statesman between Shang and Zhou dynasties. Legend has it that he left the tyrannical rule of Shang Dynasty's King Zhou and came to the territory of Zhou State, ready to assist the widely popular Zhou Count, Ji Chang. He went fishing by Wei River, but unlike other people, he did not fish with a bent hook, but with a straight hook, and his hook was a meter above the water. He explained to bewildered people that what he fished for was not fish but the king and marquis. Thus he attracted the attention of Ji Chang, and was entrusted with important task. He assisted Zhou King Wu (Ji Fa), the son of Ji Chang in annihilating Shang Dynasty and founding Western Zhou Dynasty.

right two heads; as "they need to eat the grass on both sides." This is a conceptual language of art to describe synchronization of time and separate space.

"Jiang Ziya's fishing" shows his full face, a half side and a full side face in three different expressions, attentive and focused while fishing; joyous wave when the fish approaching the bait; and a broad smile when catching the fish. It is an integration of time and space at a fishing scene, the same conceptual art as in "Herd Grazing."

Totem Structure

The tiger image created by folk artists is not the natural image of a tiger at a specific time and place; it is a surreal conceptual tiger, a totem that protects the community. For example, the chubby, short-legged "Loving tiger" is meant to keep an eye on the kids and play with them. The tiger in "A tiger coming down the mountain" showing a fierce-looking tiger with his four feet at full length is for safeguarding the residence. They are

Folk paper-cut "A tiger descending from the mountain" (Ansai, Shaanxi).

Folk paper-cut "Ai tiger" (loving tiger) (Ansai, Shaanxi).

not tigers in a natural form. In the early 1980s, China National Fine Art Institute invited six elder women from northern Shaanxi and eastern Gansu to demonstrate paper-cutting in class. When they first arrived, I wanted to show them around Beijing. They wanted to go to Beijing Zoo and see a real tiger, something they had never seen even after cutting paper tigers for a lifetime. They rushed to the tiger mountain and gazed at the real tigers without a blink of an eye. At night, they stayed up all night trying to make a paper-cut tigers in various postures from what they saw. However, having never learnt sketch, they didn't do too well, as, after all, those are two different art categories.

Paper-cut "A snake twinning round a rabbit" (Ansai, Shaanxi).

Paper-cut "A snake twining round a rabbit" and "A coiling snake" are also patron totem images, not natural snake postures. The image of a coiling snake with its head and tail crossed implies the connection of heaven and earth. Holding a mugwort in the mouth also shows that it is a legendary snake. The rabbit in the middle means that the children are bred and protected by the clan. The first "coiling snake" image was seen on painted pottery plate unearthed from Taosi Xia-Dynasty (2070–1600 BC) cultural relics in Xiangfen, Shanxi; then on the bronze ware from the Zhou Dynasty (1046–256 BC). This totem symbol has been passed down from generation to generation for over 5,000 years.

Paper-cut "Baby with coiled hair" (Ansai, Shaanxi).

Through the transformation of a totem frog, to a frog with a human face, then to humanized fairy "Baby with coiled hair," we can see the development in the shaping of this art image. There are two types of "Baby with coiled hair" in northern Shaanxi. The pa-

Nüwa Creates Humankind

Nüwa was the goddess of creation in China's mythology of remote ages. According to legend, there were no human beings when the heaven and earth came into being. She took yellow clay, mixed it with water, and molded the mixture into humankinds according to her own image, and gave them life. Later after she became very tired in the process, she made the yellow clay into slurry. So instead of hand crafting each figure, she dipped a rope in slurry and flicked it so blobs of slurry landed everywhere; each of these blobs became a common person. Persons crafted out of clay became noble and wealthy people, while persons made from slurry became poor and humble people. Nüwa not only created humankind, but also established marriage system for men and women to marry each other and produce offspring. As a result, she is also worshipped as goddess of marriage.

tron fairy totem who wears double coils, which sometimes are decorated with two roosters (indicating the sun and the moon); in a standing posture with both arms stretching upward, or holding two roosters in her hands, or one rooster (the sun) and one rabbit (the moon). If she lies on her stomach, it is the "crawling baby" on pillow case. The outline of this fairy with coiled hair is transformed from a totem frog, the first maternal ancestor of Chinese, Nüwa, in ancient historical fairy tale who made clay figures and started the Chinese nationality. The second type is the "Happy baby" who is also in a standing posture, wearing lotus flower in her hair, with both hands drooping by her sides, squatting on her heels as if giving birth. On her feet is a pair of fish. The "Happy baby" is an art image of the proliferation fairy. Research shows that in primitive society, giving birth was in a squatting position.

Timeless Structure

In folk art, art decoration features using live figures

Paper-cut "Ancient temple," decorated with peony title roof (Huangling, Shaanxi).

Folk paper-cut "Fish" (Huangling, Shaanxi).

Farmers' painting "Apple orchard" (Luochuan, Shaanxi).

like plants and animals, or natural symbols, in place of lifeless lines, black and white, and contrast variations. As we have seen in some art works, the ball in "two dragons playing with a ball" is the head of a legendary pig; peony flower replaces lifeless roof tiles; lotus flower is used in place of fish scale to decorate fish; flower and animal figures are common decorations for human clothes or animal fur, etc. Such art decoration highlights the life in the universe with luxuriant flowers and grass, joyous people and soaring horses. Such characteristics of Chinese folk art are the product of the philosophical and aesthetical outlook of the creators as a community, and their emotional and psychological qualities. Transformed decoration is not an unique feature of Chinese folk art. It can be found in different sects of Western modern art. Matisse's naked dance was a transformed figure of human body, and the transformed "Man in Clothes" still followed the law of the clothes lines in their natural forms; cubist Georges Braque's transformed human figure

Paper-cut art work "Horse" by Gao Fenglian (Yanchuan, Shaanxi).

used block shading technique. But in Western painting, there is no sign of decorative technique using peony eyes; lotus flower fish scale; or baby animals inside an abdomen; peony flower roof tile, etc. The key point here is not the transformed decoration, it is how and what is being transformed. In Western cultural concept, transformed decoration is lifeless and follows the pattern of nature; whereas with Eastern culture, it is a conceptual transformation featuring ubiquitous life decoration.

Granny Wang Lanpan's husband is an expert apple grower. He was the first man in northern Shaanxi to grow apples there some 60 years ago. Theirs was the first apple orchard on the Loess Plateau. Granny Wang's paper-cut "Apple orchard" depicts consecutive scenes from spring ploughing in the orchard; to apple transplanting and autumn harvesting and packaging into baskets. It covered all seasons, including different time and space and the entire production process. However, she still felt something missing. She was finally satisfied by adding on the top a dragon, a phoenix, and some small animal figures. Including unrelated animals like phoenix and dragon would be unthinkable in creative art of a fixed visual space and time. With folk artists, the art is to create and display a surreal world of the universe. They can add in their works anything from heaven to earth, from flower, grass to animals, to make it full of vigor and life.

In folk paper-cuts, a symbolic character "Wan" in a rotating pattern is usually added to the tail of

"Rooster" wearing a "cloud hook" (Ansai, Shaanxi).

male or *yang* animals like the ox, the tiger, the horse, the dog and the goat. It is not the natural way that these animals' tails rotate. Another example is the "cloud hook," or a "Sheng," also a male symbol, on the back of roosters as the wings.

"Dragon Boat Festival": an art form depicting the eyes as the sun without being sheltered by the eye lids (Ansai, Shaanxi).

Instead of using symbols, Gao Fenglian in Yanchuan, northern Shaanxi, incorporated the character "Wan" into her paper-cut, making the four legs of the totem animal turn into a shape of character "Wan." To display perpetuity of life in rotating posture other than adding a symbol on the tail carries even greater visual impact and special artistic appeal.

Another folk artist, Cao Dianxiang, drew a large multi-color rooster that filled up the entire paper, vigorous-looking and in bright colors. I asked her why she drew only one big rooster. She said that to be big was to be strong and powerful. I asked why she drew such a big crest. "Big rooster always has a big crest." "What about the tail, and such strong legs?" "Big rooster has huge tail, and strong, hairy legs! It crows too." The generosity and the vigor shown in their art works are representative of Chinese national spirit and the emotional and psychological qualities of the Chinese community. It would be hard to find pessimistic, sentimental art works full of self-absorbency and self-admiration which are common occurrence among the works by professional artists.

When depicting human or animal eyes, they always draw a round eyeball right in the center of the eye white, without any sheltering by the eye lids. They believed that it made the eye look bright and full of life. The embroidered rats always have three colorful lines out of the eyes known as "three stitches." It is a custom to liken the eye to the sun and the lines to sun rays.

When we were in the class in the Chinese Fine Art Institute, a graduate student created a large paper-cut in the theme of birth, marriage and death. At an art work open house, our guest grannies all disagreed to include death in it. One said, "Don't let him die. Keep him alive to serve the people." Another student copied a model of Granny Hu Fenglian's paper-cut "The Rooster," but left out the symbol "Sheng" or the "cloud hook", as unnecessary. Granny Hu said, "You can leave out other parts, but not the 'sheng,' because that is the symbol of life, the heart and the soul of this art work." These words provided us some good "food" for thought.

The Structure of Colors

The color structure in Chinese folk art is based on the view of perpetual life; *yin-yang*; and the five elements in terms of time and space.

Color Preference and the Evolution of Life

Red is a legendary color idolized by the Chinese community. As early as forty thousand years ago, the Upper Cave Man spread red mineral powder along side the dead to pray for spiritual eternity and perpetual life. Today, red is still the symbol of life. The red color idol is rooted in the worship of nature, the sun, fire, and human blood which is a symbol of human's own

Wedding ceremony (Huaxian County, Shaanxi).

life. At the end of a long night, it is the red sun rising from the east that brings everything back to life. Where there is a red sun, fire and warm blood, there is life. On Chinese New Year, people are like waves of a red ocean. Many are dressed in red, red blouse, red hat, or red all over. Huge red character of happiness, antithetical couplets and red fire works are everywhere, creating a joyous, festive mood. Red is also the color to dispel evil. Life-threatening ghosts and devils are all scared of red. Therefore, cinnabar and bright red paper became the legend color for Chinese.

Color Preference in *Yin-yang*

For Chinese, red and white are colors for life and death. Red is for celebrating wedding and giving birth; and white for funeral and memorial services for those who passed away at old age. They are referred to as red and white ceremonies. The preference came from the warm red color of the sun and white snow in withering cold. At wedding ceremony, male wear red and woman dress in green as "the red official and the

Funeral (Baiyangdian, Hebei).

green lady," an unity of the red sun and green earth which bear grass and crops. Different nationality has its own color preference in *yin-yang* thought. The tiger totem nation who regards black tiger as heaven and the father; and white tiger as earth and the mother, uses black and white as the colors for heaven and earth, *yin* and *yang*, male and female.

Color Preference for the Five Elements and the Eight Diagrams

In the community, Chinese defines color composition by the five

"Pyramid-shaped dumpling" winded around with colorful threads "glutinous rice dumpling" to drive away evil spirits on the Dragon Boat Festival (Qingyang, Gansu).

elements, which reflects their comprehension of time and space in the universe. The five elements, east, west, south, north and center, compose the space. Each element has a designated color; the base color of east is dark blue; west is white; south is red; north is black; and center is yellow. The four seasons, spring, summer, autumn and winter that rotate all year long, correspond to the colors of the five elements. Dark blue is for spring; red for summer; yellow for long summer, white for autumn and black for winter; corresponding to five totem animals, are dark blue dragon of the east; white tiger of the west; red sparrow of the south; black turtle of the north and central yellow; corresponding to humanized legendary god, are dark blue emperor of the east, white emperor of the west; red emperor of the south; black emperor of

Conditional color structure in traditional western painting oil on canvass.

Color structure of Chinese painting based on the original color of the object.

Yin-yang and the five elements color structure in Chinese folk art (Ansai, Shaanxi).

the north and yellow emperor of the central region; corresponding to the five elements of gold, timber, water, fire and earth, are dark blue timber, white gold, red fire, black water and yellow earth.

The base of traditional color composition in Western art is determined by the reflection of natural light, with cold and warm colors in an opposite unity. Change of light is the basis of color application in Western color structure.

The color composition of Chinese paintings is based on the original color of the objects. The color composition of Chinese folk art is based on the visual image of the objects and philosophical comprehension of *yin-yang* and the five elements definition.

Creators of Chinese Folk Art

The creators of Chinese folk art come from millions of labourers among the People. They include both "the dexterous-hands" who engage in agricultural labour and the folk crafts-persons who bave been completely or partly out of the agricultural labor. These folk artists have contributed to the handing-down and development of the Chinese culture through their works.

The Art of the Laborer Community

The creator of Chinese folk art is the working class community. Over several thousand years, Chinese society was based on natural economy of farming, animal husbandry, fishing and hunting. The labor division in the society placed men in the field and construction work, leaving women in charge of house work and custom cultural and art activities. The rural female workers formed the majority of this art community. Using the most basic tools like a pair of scissors and a needle, they created a variety of art works going from one generation to the next, greatly contributing to the heritage of original Chinese culture. Special credit is given to those elderly women, the illiterate grandmothers who take care of every-day household works in China's rural areas. They are the

The daughter-in-law of the nameless paper-cut crackajack in Ansai, Shaanxi, Yan Xifang's family.

Late paper-cut expert Qi Xiumei from Zhen Yuan, Gansu (named as master of Chinese folk art in paper-cut), coaching her grandchild to make paper-cut for window decoration.

owners, creators and carriers of original Chinese culture. Issues that had been disputed for years in the literature and art circles were unraveled by them in a few words. In northern Shaanxi, many of those grandmothers were born inside the cave, lived and raised their families there, and then passed away peacefully in the cave. For a life time, they decorated their cave with a full range of art works of their own, expressing their understandings and their emotions. Their cave is like a miniature world of the universe, filled with people

Wang Lanpan and her family.

Rural female paper-cut expert Ku Shulan cutting window decoration flower in her residence cave. She was named Master of Chinese Arts and Crafts by UNESCO.

laughing, horse roaring, birds soaring and fish jumping. It is a living museum of the original ecological culture.

In old China, rural women did not have any social status. This grandmother in Nuanshuiquan, Ansai of northern Shaanxi, did not even have a name of her own. People referred her with her daughter-in-law's name Yan Xifang. She lived to 81 years of age and died in 1997. In her last days, leaning against her daughter-in-law, she managed to change all the window and door decorations in the cave with new paper-cuts she made. Large horizontal border flowers were along the wall above the brick bed; black kitchen range was decorated with beautiful egg shells. Before she died, she handed over to her daughter-in-law a stack of original paper-cut patterns and said solemnly, "I have nothing to leave you. I have loved cutting out window flowers all my life. It is my last wish to leave these patterns for you to keep." There are similar stories in other families too. They are the true folk artists.

There are many female laborer artists in the rural areas. In 1970

Ping-pong Diplomacy

Ping-pong Diplomacy refers to the event of China's invitation of the United States table tennis players to visit China. It happened at the time of Cold War. China and the United States had no established diplomatic relations. To improve the relations between the two countries and promote the friendly communications between people of the two countries, China took advantage of the 31st World Table Tennis Championship held in Japan and voluntarily invited the U.S. Table Tennis Team to visit China for a friendly contest in 1971..This initiative met a positive response from the United States. Three months after the visit to China by the U.S. Table Tennis Team, Dr. Kissinger, Assistant to the U.S. President for National Security Affairs, paid a secret visit to China. The subsequent frequent exchanges between the United States and China finally led to the successful establishment of diplomatic relations in 1979. Acclaimed "the small ball that turns on the large ball," "Ping-pong Diplomacy" serves as a successful example of developing diplomatic relations through ingenious employment of external force.

when I was working in Yan'an Mass Art Museum in northern Shaanxi, we conducted a survey on cultural art in 13 counties and cities. Take Ansai County for example where we went through every single household, among a population of fifty-thousand, over half were female; and twenty-thousand of them were in the age group that could make paper-cut, embroidery, or floury flower. Some 5,000 were considered capable hand and 250 were outstanding. We selected 40 persons as excellent candidates and called them the "seeded players." (It was at the time of U.S.-China Ping-pong Diplomacy. Seeded players were selected for ping-pong match.) Only two out of 40 were under age 40. Later in 1980, in my nation-wide research of rural culture, I had similar statistics in other parts of the country.

Those elderly women are owners of the authoritative folk art, folk customs. With a pair of scissors in hand, they are experts in paper-cutting; picking up a needle and thread, they are excellent in embroidery work; they are also superb cooks in making floury flowers, and they

Women of Bai ethnic group working on wax printing (Dali, Yunnan).

Design of wax printing.

can also paint when picking up a brush too. They are good house-wives at home, and capable hands in farm fields. As the folk say-ing goes, "A capable hand in one thing is capable in all." At age 4 or 5, they started to learn paper-cutting from their mothers, and practiced for decades till senior age, laying solid foundations in art image styling; at young age they learnt embroidery skills from their mothers and made embroidery undergarment, pillow case, shoe soles, cigarette bags, needle holders, and developed deep-seated appreciation for coloring; they knead floury flowers, jujube moun-tains at Chinese New Year and cold swallow on the Pure Bright-

Women in the rural area along the Yellow River reaches making floury flower "cold swallow" on the Pure Brightness Day.

ness Festival, year after year, well trained on three-dimensional art styling. Through a lifetime practice, they are well versed in traditional art patterns which have been passed down for centuries. Every Spring Festival they will make window paper-cutting and circular flower pattern to decorate their cave houses. During the Pure Brightness Festival they will do dough modeling and cold swallow. In leisure time, they will embroider belly covers for their husbands, shoe flowers and pillow flowers for themselves and tiger patterns for their children. They will make tiger shoes and tiger pillows. Whenever wedding ceremony is held in the village, they will offer help by cutting out cluster flowers and angular flowers for the arrangement of the bridal chamber. They will make hand-in-hand melon dolls and paste them on the door lintels to ward off the monsters and evils. When the rainy and cloudy spell lasts for too long, they will cut out sky-sweeping nanny, tie it to the head of a pole, and erect the pole in the courtyard so that the nanny will sweep away the cloud and rain away for them. They are fully entitled to a group of well accomplished folk artists.

The Art of Folk Artist Community

Career folk artists are creators who engage in folk art to make a living. They are already separated, or semi-separated, from farmland work. Career folk artist is still part of the laborer community; however, their art is no longer for self service, but a service for

Folk artist carving shadow show figures (Huaxian County, Shaanxi).

social life. Outstanding rural female artists who still engage in farmland work are not career folk artists. Their excellent achievement in art work has earned them, along with career folk artists, praises from the society as folk artists or masters of folk art. However, they are still not career folk artists.

In a span of over 2,000 years of farming economy, China's commodity economy gradually developed in its own pace. In areas where commodity economy and culture were more developed, some folk art creators started to detach from the original community to make a living by way of producing creative folk art works. A new group emerged as career folk artist. Consisting mostly male, career folk artists engaged in either sole proprietary or cooperative business, including family business. In order to make a living, they needed to produce the maximum quantity, and meet the taste and the trend of the society in content, category and art form. As a result, changes were made from the material; to the tools, even the art work itself. To achieve the quantity, burin replaced scissors, and paper-cutting transformed into paper carving. Needless to say, the change of

Folk artist making exorcist dance and ritual masks (Pingxiang, Jiangxi).

A woodcut New Year picture printing shop racing to produce kitchen god picture (Kaifeng, Henan).

tools altered the style and the features of the art works. Career artists' carving technique is peerless. With ultimate precision and delicacy, their works are among the most exquisite fine art ever created. The paper carvings produced by career folk artists are categorized in two groups; the works that mostly maintained the original folk paper-cut both in theme features and art forms, however, with more refined craftsmanship; and the works largely influenced by the literati and professional artists, shifting both the content and the theme features of folk art works to the style of Chinese painting, mainly

A family workshop making wood carving toys (Tancheng, Shandong).

Folk artist putting on facial make-ups for folk play "Mu Lian rescuing her mother" (Luxi, Hunan).

depicting theatrical figures, mountains and rivers; flowers-and-birds, classic chambers and pagodas, with first-class craftsmanship and elegant style.

Career folk artists who have completely separated or semi-separated from farmland work, are the main creators of a wide range of commercial folk art works including woodcut New Year picture; leather silhouette; puppets; exorcist-play mask; wax printing, dyeing and weaving; tapestry and Xinjiang carpet; funeral origami; kite; toy; stone carving; and graving.

Various Chinese Folk Art Works

Rooted in the original Chinese philosophy and social customs, nourished by cultures from diverse nationalities, geographical localities and through different historical times, Chinese folk art has now blossomed and laden with fresh fruit, which have a history dating back a long time, more vibrant than ever before.

Chinese folk art features multiple categories; therefore, it would be hard to cover all. Following are exemplary few. Among the many art works by Chinese female laborers, we will focus on paper-cut (paper-cut also serves as patterns for embroidery, and plane views for floury flower); and for the works by career folk artists which is male-dominant, we will cover leather silhouette, woodcut New Year picture, an exorciser's mask, and kite.

Paper-cut

Of all folk art works, paper-cut is the most participated. Often characterized by geographical regions, paper-cut is rich with historical and cultural heritage. Even though it has only been 2,000 years since the invention of paper, the cultural implication and art forms that paper-cut represents goes back all the way to primitive society 6,000–7,000 years ago. The cultural value it carries far exceeds the value of art itself; it enriches the entire original Chinese art system, art formation and color structure, having deep impact on philosophy, aesthetics, history, ethnology, sociology and anthropology.

As a cultural carrier of the original Chinese philosophy, paper-cut is embodied in all aspects of folk custom and culture. They are

Traditional folk paper-cut "Water vase for the tree of life" (Shandong).

in the forms of window decoration; border flower for brick bed; cave-vault flower; totem door god; daily life appliance such as vat and jar flower, porcelain decorations; dress and adornment like embroidery, hat decoration, shoe flower, pillow case and under-garment decorative patterns; and for wedding ceremony; memo-rial service; birthday celebration, etc. There are also pillow case with paper-cut patterns featuring tiger, doll or fish, symbolic of birth from totem mother's body; and "*Yin-yang* fish;" "Fish biting lotus;" "Lotus bearing seeds;" for marriage and multiplication; "The tree of life" symbolizing eternity of spirit and continuation of life at funeral and burial ceremonies; holiday paper-cut "A buckled bowl;" "Rat bit open the sky;" indicating that when heaven and earth connect, all things come back to life, propagation of children and harvesting crops. In the first lunar month, to welcome the be-ginning of spring ploughing, paper-cut "Spring cow" is pasted on the door for safeguard; at Pure Brightness Festival, paper-cut "Fotuo" is placed on the ancestor's tomb (Manchu); and in the fifth Lunar month, on the Dragon Boat Festival, people use "Love ti-ger" paper-cut as a talisman to drive away vicious spirit and disease. In folk customs, there are "Baby with coiled hair" and a variety of its transformed figures as patron saint and propagation fairy; Miao ethnic group's legendary figures paper-cut on the "pounding cows" altar for the ancestors; and paper-cut featuring exorcist figures and festivities, etc.

Folk paper-cut is a living fossil of art history. The cultural heri-tage it carries corresponds with the cultural antiques unearthed from the same area and with the historical documentation and leg-endary stories. For example, one of the three influential tribes in ancient history is Miao group inhabited along the Yangtze River. About 4,500 years ago, Miao strode northward and waged a war with Huaxia tribal group along the Yellow River basin. After being defeated, they retreated to live in the enclosed southwest moun-tain area. Today's Miao and Yao ethnic groups in Yunnan Province are their descendants. Without a written language, Miao ethnic group had no documentation other than verbal legendary stories. However, the living paper-cut of their national dress vividly depicts the legendary story from the birth of Miao ethnic group to the migration journey after the battle. It is like a complete ancient history book of Miao ethnic group. And the paper-cut patterns of the embroidery dress still popular along the Yellow River today is like a history book of the ancient totem culture, displaying totem idols from images of animal totem; to half animal, half human; and humanized totem.

Chinese folk paper-cut embodies a complete system of philosophy, which was not based on the philosophy of Confucianism, Taoism or other schools of thought. It was based on the original Chinese philosophy and art system from prehistorical time. Some paper-cut designs fully conformed to the patterns on the painted pottery from prehistorical time that it helped bring out the meaning of silent symbols. For example, "A pair of fish with human face" (on painted pottery from 6,000-year-old Yangshao Culture) was not a natural fish. It was a cultural code in prehistorical philosophy. The same logic applies to Chinese New Year paper-cut "A buckled bowl;" and "An unbuckled bowl with a rat coming out;" and "the rat bites open the sky." In China, rat is the god of proliferation. "The rat bites open the sky" symbolizes the unity of *yin-yang* and propagation in the universe. Other examples like to surpass time and space in a feature painting; drawing two eyes on a profile based on conceptual views; and a bowl with an arc top and a flat bottom to symbolize the round sky and square earth; are all featured art displays of the original Chinese philosophy.

With a vast territory and multi-ethnic population, Chinese folk paper-cut bears distinct national and geographical features. In art style, northern China is more straightforward, unconstraint, and broad minded; while in the south, it is more exquisite and delicate, full of delight and witty. From the creators, the rural female folk

Paper-cut "The tree of life with baby with coiled hair and a pair of tigers" (Zhenyuan, Gansu).

artists use only a pair of scissors and paper to convey their conceptual figures and color effect which surpass time and space; while male-dominant career artists make paper carvings with superb delicacy and graciousness in a more realistic style and art language. From the functionality in social life, paper-cut for embroidery patterns are given more emphasis on the outline for decorativeness; while cave window decoration gives more delicacy to the inner pattern to let in light. I marveled at the delicacy of the window paper-cuts in Jiaodong area, Shandong, that had lines as fine as gossamer. In general art style, each art work brings out an unique, personal touch of the author. Shaanxi female artist Ku Shulan's multi-layer, multi-color paper-cut composite is an elegant, huge piece of art work; Hebei career folk artist Wang Laoshang created a singular paper carving series featuring theatrical figures, each with distinguished personality, clear-cut outline and in beautiful colors.

The tools and raw materials used by Chinese women folk artists are a pair of scissors, a needle and a piece of rough paper. However, over 2,000 years in the course of history, they've created an art with unique features and power-ful expressiveness which is matchless in many ways. The sim-plicity of the tools and the raw materials they used; the implica-tion these art works convey; the massive participation and the functional features; all contribute to its special value. Even in re-mote mountain areas where pa-

Paper-cut "Bird with fish in the mouth" for pillow case patterns (Ansai, Shaanxi).

per supply is scarce, paper-cut still plays an active role in custom festivities including holiday and birthday celebrations; wedding and memorial services; residential building decorations and social custom activities.

In the Astana tomb in Turpan, Xingjiang, excavated five paper-cuts originated in the 5th century, Northern and Southern Dynas-ties (420–589). They were pairing monkeys, sheep, deer and but-terflies and ball flowers. 1500 years later, the same paper-cut de-sign is still very popular along the Silk Road in Gansu and Shaanxi.

Excavated from the Tang tombs in Astana, Turpan, Xingjiang, were seven hand-in-hand "Baby with coiled hair" paper-cuts ly-ing on a paper incarnation of the owner. Using paper folding fig-ure in place of absent body of military generals who died in battle field was meant to revive the spirit of the dead. In rural areas of Baishui and Pengya, Shaanxi, folk custom paper-cut still uses this "Baby with coiled hair" in a row holding hands to dispel bad luck and cure disease, with the exact same cultural implication and so-cial function as that of over a thousand years ago.

Paper-cut also serves as a way to identify cultural characteristics of various ethnic groups. Miao ethnic group's paper-cut told the story of their totem ancestor, the butterfly mother changed from a maple tree, and paired with the water bubble to give birth to Jiang Yang and Lei Gong, along with the dragon, the tiger, the snake, the elephant, the buffalo and the centipede. After a flood, Jiang Yang married his sister and started human propagation. Xinjiang Uygur ethnic group's paper pattern for embroidery is a composite of the tree of life and the sun; or a water jar or a bottle as the transformed tree of life; in central Shaanxi old Qiang ethnic group cultural birthplace, embroidery patterns are tiger totem pillow cases, tiger head shoes and undergarments, and tiger vests to keep down the five poisonous.

The skills and techniques in folk art paper-cut are shown in various ways. In rural northern China which is long time enclosed but self-sufficient, small-scale peasant economy prevails, women make paper-cut for a life time with nothing but a pair of scissors and raw paper. Their knowledge and skills in the art of paper-cut perfected through practice. From small window flowers to large-scale art works of 5–6 meters long, without a draft, they pick up a pair of scissors and start cutting at will, showing great confidence and skills as masters of art. Along southeast of the Yangtze River, capitalist commodity economy first started in the Southern Song Dynasty which brought about the town culture and career folk artists. To meet the need of the newly emerged folk customs, commodity market system and town-culture aesthetics, folk art grew into a style of multi-layer paper engraving art with highly skilled carving and color painting techniques. Highly talented art masters and artists from all backgrounds have created a wide range of art works such as mountains and waters; gardens and courtyards, birds and flowers, grass and insects, and human figures. These quintessential art works with true-to-life depictions of the subjects are different from those made by rural women in north China.

Among all Chinese folk paper-cut, the most popular and largely embedded in folk customs are dragon light origami for festivals; paper-cutting and origami for funeral and memorial services; exorcist dance and plays; and Miao ethnic group's "pounding cow" ceremony to worship ancestors.

As a historical cultural heritage, folk paper-cut still exists today but only in China and Mexico. It has basically disappeared from other parts of the world. In Mexico, only the paper burial objects to worship ancestors, similar to China's Pure Brightness Day, is still popular. When I was on a research tour in France in early 1980s, the paper-cut still available there were from professional artists and art masters. The old-time widely participated folk paper-cut was all history. Among the 40 folk custom museums I visited, there were only two folk paper-cut works kept in the save at a small town museum near Orleans. They were not displayed for fear of getting damaged. The same situation was true in other countries. Paper-cut by professional artists are still around, but no more folk paper-cut. Of the four countries in the world whose civilizations date to ancient times, China is the only one that still actively practices the folk art of paper-cutting, which is now a major cultural

Totem paper-cut "Deer horn flower" for Chinese New Year (Xinjiang, Shanxi).

heritage of the mankind; and its continued preservation demands urgent attention.

Leather Silhouette

Telling stories of the ancient times over a curtain frame; playing music and beating drums under the stage light; the music conveys joy and sorrow, partings and reunion in life; and the show reveals the crafty and the evil in the past. Three feet of raw silk makes the show, jokes and humor slip through figure tips; one voice tells stories of a thousand years and two hands display the battle ground. One piece of leather creates joy and sorrow, laughter and anger; and a profile contains royalty, betrayal, virtue and evil." This is a true portrayal of the leather silhouette which combines in one literature, theatre, music, and fine art. The shadow show props and characters are the key areas of creative art.

Chinese leather silhouette show has numerous names featured by its locality. It is the "Shadow show" in Shaanxi; "Luanzhou shadow" in Hebei; "Donkey leather silhouette" in Northeast China; "Light shadow show" in Sichuan, "Leather Nannan" in Guangdong; "Whipping monkey" or "Monkey show" in Fujian and Taiwan.

Leather silhouette and puppet shows are the earliest and most popular stage plays in Chinese puppet theatrical art. At all custom occasions such as holidays and festivals; flower fairs or temple fairs; spring worship and autumn requital; chasing away disasters and inviting fortune; red and white celebrations; child birth and career promotion; a stage is set up in the village to put on shows, singing and dancing. Theatrical troupe is usually headed by someone who owns the costume; or a family troupe consisting members of the same household. Some shows are series shows that can go on for 7 or 8 nights, even as long as two weeks; others are single show or the highlights from series shows. Some troupes would set up puppet shows during the day and make shadow shows at night. There is always a pre-show episode to salute gods. On wedding ceremonies, celebrating child birth or first full month of the newborns, the show on will be "sending off proliferation fairy;" birthday celebration for the elderly is the "three stars—fortune, wealth and longevity;" erecting roof beam for new houses is "Lu Ban carpenter show;" and at Rev. Guan's temple fair or at prayer time to seek protection against disasters and pestilence, it is "Rev. Guan Yu, the all-time evil conqueror." The size of shadow show troupes average from 5–8 members, some with only two. Shadow show actors are still involved in field work. They travel around the neighboring villages when field work is idle, carrying costumes on their shoulders, or on donkey backs, to set up temporary stages. Traditional screen is a wooden frame about one meter high by two meters wide, covered over with white sheet. It is called the "shadow window" or the "bright spot" by the folks. With oil lamps hanging over the screen box, actors and actress manipulate the post of silhouette figures against the cloth screen window, singing along to the music accompaniment. With brilliant skills and amazing techniques, and through those shadow figures, stage settings and costumes cast on the screen by the lamp light, they present various roles and plots with vivid performance. Action scenes have intense fighting between warriors, reining horses before falling swords; drama show is unfolded with genuine emotions, singing in tearful voices at highlights. Audience

Process of making leather silhouette show figures (Huaxian County, Shaanxi).

An action leather silhouette show put on by Luannan leather silhouette troupe, Hebei.

under the stage is deeply captured by the plot and the performance.

Traditional shadow figure is about 35 cm high, mostly made of cow skin (Shaanxi, Shanxi, Gansu, Qinghai, Henan, Hubei, Sichuan and Yunnan), or donkey skin (Hebei, Inner Mongolia, three provinces in Northeast, and Shandong), and painted goat skin (Zhejiang and Guangdong). In Jiangxi and Hunan, it is made with carved paper sandwiched with color fabric. Most leather silhouette artists were experienced senior artists with specialties handed down in the family. They went through complicated process from leather selecting, processing, engraving, coloring and painting, to sewing and assembling. After that, they added a neck sheathe to insert wig to complete the 11 movable components (the head, the upper and lower shoulders, the upper body and the lower body, and two legs) before assembling them onto three bamboo sticks, one fixed and two movable, for the neck and two hands. Depending on the role, one figure could have as many as four sets of wigs. For a large show, with male, female, painted face and clown four categories of

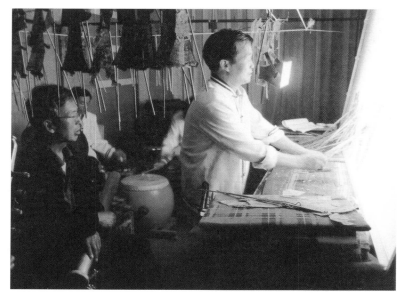

Back stage scene of a drama shadow show, with mostly singing and story telling, by a troupe in Gansu.

some 80 figures, it might have as many as four hundred wigs. In addition, they carried almost everything from tables and chairs; vehicles and horses; general's tent, carriage and boat; palace and chambers; Buddhist and Taoist temples, to the background stage arrangement for the sky, earth and water. With these costumes, they could put on some 100–200 different shows.

Regular shadow figure head is a full profile, known as "half face." Clown and villain sometimes are given half profile, called "70% face;" fairies and Buddha are shown with a full face. Shadow figure's body is mostly 70%. Carving of shadow figures is very particular. It requires using knife with ease and making turns smoothly. The hollowed-out facial outline, in particular, requires an exceptional skill in craftsmanship, making lines as thin as "stretching wires," sharp and translucent. Body figure using chisel engraving has a variety of designs, including snow flake, charac-ter "Wan" shape, wealth and fortune, wintersweets, fish scale, pine needle and star eyes, etc. Leather silhouette coloring is usually bright and transparent, mostly in black, red, yellow, and green. Music accompaniment are four string and south string instrument; bowed instrument; four-string moon-shaped instrument; drum; gong; flute; hand allegro; and horn. Based on geographical localities, each place has its own unique style and characteristics in shadow figure design, music and instrument.

China boasts a long art history of leather silhouette show, originate in Chinese Taoist's astrology, in the Han Dynasty (206 BC–220 AD). The earliest record found was a moving love story. Having missed his deceased wife Lady Li, Emperor Han Wudi invited a necromancer to dinner, asking him to call back Lady Li's spirit. The necromancer put up curtains at night, lit candle light to create shadow figures. Seemingly the emperor saw Lady Li's face again and he missed her even more.

The Tang Dynasty (618–907), along with the introduction of Indian Buddhism in the late years of the Eastern Han Dynasty, Buddhists set up altars for night seminars along the Silk Road and Chang'an, the then capital of the Tang Dynasty and its political and economical center, preaching Buddhist scriptures and telling stories in the form of chanting and singing with illustrations of series of pictures. Chinese Taoist also preached Taoist scriptures and Taoism, following the Tang Dynasty's Taoist melody and instrument, with simple rhythmic accompaniment. As of today,

Cattle hide leather silhouette introduced to Egypt from China during the Yuan Dynasty. Photo taken at Berlin Museum, Germany.

Cattle hide leather silhouette from Hubei (Qing Dynasty).

shadow shows in western Shaanxi, eastern Gansu and southern Shanxi still follow the same way of chanting and storytelling. Buddhist and Taoist scripture-preaching with illustration later developed into using paper partitions and light to create shadows on the paper along with storytelling. In Huaxian County, Shaanxi Province, shadow show is still referred to as "storytelling behind the paper partition." Huaxian County was known as "bowl tunes," which was also named after the clock-like bronze percussion instrument from Indian Buddhist.

In the Northern Song Dynasty (960–1127), with the development of the commodity economy, recreational activities of folk singing and chanting flourished. Chinese shadow show changed from entertaining god to entertaining people; from

Cattle hide leather silhouette from Shaanxi Xilu (Ming Dynasty).

preaching scriptures to telling history stories, reaching to a level of unprecedented prosperity. Recorded in *Dong Jing Meng Hua Lu* (Dreaming of the Flourishing East Capital) by Meng Yuanlao in the Song Dynasty, "On the night of 16ᵗʰ in the first lunar month, a music canopy was set up at every gate in the capital city Bianliang (Kaifeng city). The streets were filled with people. On the street where no music canopy was seen, there were small shadow show canopies. No matter what the weather was like, crowds of people congregated inside the canopy day after day." In the book *Event Narration* by Gao Cheng of the Song Dynasty, it reads, "During the time of Renzong, shadow show 'The Three Kingdoms' was on in the capital city which attracted the wealthy families. Audience shed tears at the scene when Guan Yu was beheaded." Leather silhouette show performance started with storytelling, then transformed to plays based on fictions, short stories, public legal case, cavalry, and history script.

In the Ming (1368–1644) and Qing (1616–1911) dynasties, China turned into a unified, prosperous country. Leather silhouette show

Cattle hide leather silhouette from Luanzhou, Hebei (Qing Dynasty).

Cattle hide leather silhouette from Shaanxi Donglu (Qing dynasty).

also gained major momentum during this period, with more exquisite carving techniques and greater variety of play types. After
the establishment of the People's Republic in 1949, plays compiled
on the basis of news story were "A White Haired Girl;" "Red Leaf
River;" "Liu Hulan;" and so on, a list of over hundred plays. The
vitality of Chinese leather silhouette show lies in its long history
and its deeply rooted base in the masses.

From the 13th–15th centuries, Chinese leather silhouette was introduced to Indonesia, Malaysia and other islands in Southeast Asia,
and then it moved west, concurrently with the expedition of the
Mongolian army, to Persian in Central Asia, Turkey in West Asia
and Egypt in North Africa. From the 17th century, Western Catho-
lic missionaries took it to Italy, Germany and France. French King
Louis the 14th at once watched a shadow show in the Versailles. In
1774, German poet Goethe recommended Chinese leather silhouette show at William exposition, and directed a shadow show on a
German story in 1781. Shadow show was then known as Chinese
shadow show.

The rapid development of modern economy in urban and rural

areas, coupled with the growing influence of television and film culture, traditional leather silhouette is almost precipitating into distinction nationwide except in a few regions in eastern Gansu and Liaoning. Now only some 200 leather silhouette troupes are still around, down from over 1,000 nationwide in the 1980s.

Woodcut New Year Picture

China is the birthplace of wood block printing, and Chinese woodcut painting, also the earliest ever invented, enjoys high reputation in the world.

Woodcut New Year picture is for the occasion of Chinese Spring Festival. It features beautiful art design with bright, delightful colors. It fits the mood of the people longing for a happy life, a

Woodcut New Year picture door god, Shen Tu and Yu Lei (Yangliuqing, Tianjin).

Woodcut picture painted door god, unearthed in 1992 in Bairin Right Banner, Inner Mongolia, and kept by Linxi County Institute for Antiques Management.

fresh start at the beginning of a year and a new cycle of perpetual life. Popular themes of New Year picture include house safeguard, family blessing, crop harvest, longevity, safety, and prosperity.

Woodcut New Year picture covers a wide range of subjects and in a variety of designs. Hanging on the door to keep the vicious spirits away are door gods (super-natural tigers, golden roosters, civil and military door gods); on the screen wall facing the door are fortune inviting; treasure keeping or a character "Fu" (Good fortune) in a square diamond shape; in the center of the main room is the central god (Zhong Kui; an official from heaven to bestow fortune; three stars of fortune, wealth and longevity); on the wall in the bedroom are entertaining and enlightening pictures or framed calligraphy strips (theatrical stories, life and folk customs, babies and pretty girls, mountains and waters, flowers and fish, as well as news stories); across the dish cabin is new-year picture used as dust proof paper; there are also pictures of history stories; patterns of lions roosters and auspicious symbols. There are also bed border flower, window decoration, table border, money hanger, kitchen horse, lamp flower, merits and virtues paper, etc., some several dozen types.

Folk New Year picture emerged in pre-historical time and was used as the door god. As a rule in social and cultural development, human awareness for door god went from the worship of natural animal, to deifier, and to humanized god. According to historical records, the custom of drawing "a rooster at house entrance; and a tiger on the door" date back in pre-historical society. In central Shaanxi, Baotou of Inner Mongolia, and Lingbao of Henan, even today, it is still a custom to paste paper-cut of a pair of tigers, or golden roosters, golden cows on the door leaves for safeguard. In northern China, woodcut New Year picture from the Ming and Qing dynasties still kept the tradition of using the deified tiger and rooster as patron saint for residence. Later on, the name of the Door God became fixed as Shen Tu and Yu Lei. The transition from deified animal to humanized god started in the Tang Dynasty when images of renowned warriors Qin Shubao and Yuchi Jingde were worshiped as the door god. As history recorded, "Great Majesty of the Tang Dynasty (Li Shimin) was miffed one night. When he was in bed, he heard the noise of throwing bricks and tiles outside, along with spooky howling. He was scared and told his subjects. Qin Shubao came forward and presented, 'I'd serve by your majesty's door in military attire with Yuchi Jingde.' He granted it. The subsequent nights went by peacefully. The emperor awarded the two generals and ordered the painting of their images to be hanged over the two gates to the palace to keep the spirits away." Later generations followed suit, making those images permanent door gods. Based on this legend, images of the two generals in military attire became a popular New Year picture as door gods ever since.

Carved line cut board for woodcut New Year picture from the Qing Dynasty (Zhuxianzhen, Henan).

China is a multi-ethnic country, and each has its own door god. The earliest door god I saw was in 1999 in Xiaocheng Village of Yanchuan in northern Shaanxi. Right in front of a residential cave was a full set of two stone carving door gods in military attire. It belonged to the northern nationality of the Northern Zhou Dynasty (557–581) 1, 300 years back. Later, I saw four color pictures hand-painted on wooden board kept by Linxi County Institute for Antiques Management, unearthed from the Liao (816–1125) tomb in 1992, also the property of northern nationality. The pictures were painted in large brush strokes with distinct national strait of the northerners. The painting was made around the same time period in history as the door god of the Song Dynasty found in the Song tomb in Henan Province.

The booming commodity economy and handicraft industry along with the advancement in wood block printing during the Song Dynasty changed the manufacture of Chinese woodcut New Year picture from mainly hand-painting to wood block printing, bringing major expansions to the New Year picture industry both in category and content. Its all-inclusive themes ranged from the then folk customs; field work and lyric life; people and country scenery; to theatrical plays and operas; children and family pedigree; magic rocks and immortal wild lives. As was recorded in *Wulin Jiushi* by

Zhou Mi of the Northern Song Dynasty, "Since last October, market place in the capital city has been filled with hardcover New Year pictures for sale, pictures of door gods large and small; peach symbols; Zhong Kui; lions; tiger heads; colorful strips and spring flowers paper-cut and all types of worship offerings."

The development in chromatographic wood block printing around the late Ming Dynasty further ignited the prosperity of woodcut picture industry. By the peak time of Qianlong and Jiaqing years in the Qing Dynasty, subjects exhibited through New Year picture expanded to include history stories; theatre plays; scenery spots; flower vases; fashion models and news figures; etc., with more mature engraving and painting techniques, as well as highly improved color application.

Reputable woodcut New Year picture manufacturing and printing shops were rampant across the country, namely, Yangliuqing in Tianjin; Taohuawu in Suzhou; Mianzhu in Sichuan; Linfen and Xinjiang in Shanxi; Zhuxianzhen in Henan; Longhui Tantou in Hunan; Pingdu, Liaocheng and Weixian in Shangdong; Wuqiang, Hebei; Zhangzhou, Fujian; Fushan, Guangdong; and Fengxiang, Shaanxi. With unique styles and features, they each held a place of its own in the forest of folk New Year picture.

An artist carving against the draft (Zhuxianzhen, Henan).

The making of woodcut picture was a package process from drafting, woodcut graving, printing, chromatography, to hand painting touch-up. First, a painter outlined the picture with ink marker and made a color effect draft and several monochromatic drafts. After that a carving specialist pasted the painting backward onto the wood sheet to carve against the draft. Carving was the highly skilled part. The line cut needed to be decisive yet smooth; sharp and superimposed; delicate and even. Each monochromatic draft had its own carved color board. Then it was ready for printing. Laying the main wood block on the counter for the first or the main draft; then changed over one by one to print the monochromatic blocks for chromatograph printing, securing the block and the paper every time to achieve the highest accuracy.

Modern woodcut New Year picture "Coin tree" (Weifang, Shandong).

In the period of Republic of China, common pigments for yellow were made from Chinese Scholar tree flower; ruby from perilla tree; and the dark smoke crust on the bottom of the cooking pot were used for black coloring. Later, imported magenta and malachite green were also used to achieve brighter color contrast. Manually processed woodcut picture only employed printing to make semi-finished products. Crucial areas like human head, face and hands were still needed hand-painted, with great emphasis on the face, eyes and eyebrows. Some facial expressions painted by experienced artists were so vivid and true-to-life that the whole picture was enhanced with their magic touch.

Masks and the Culture of Exorcism

Pingxiang along the mid-stream of the Yangtze River is a border area of Hunan and Jiangxi provinces, situated right in between of the Dongting Lake and the Poyang Lake. In 1980s, when I set my foot onto this part of the world, I encountered an overwhelming, massive exorcist culture, with a general's statue every 5 *li*; and an

Exorcist activities at an exorcist temple (Pingxiang, Jiangxi).

exorcist temple every 10 *li*. I felt like being in an ancient world of totem culture and the center of a tribal culture. Sima Qian recorded in *Shi Ji* (Historical Records), "Old time Miao tribe had Dongting on the left and Pengli on the right." The place he referred to was right along the border area of Hunan and Jiangxi, the birthplace of Miao-Li tribal culture headed by Chiyou in the ancient times.

Unearthed in 1989 from a commercial tomb in Xin'gan, Jiangxi Province, the bronze mask with ox horns and protruding teeth on a human face; and the pottery mask from the close-by Qingjiang Wu relics;

both fitted in with the totem image of Chiyou described as having a "bronze head with horns" in the historical records. It was also the image of the "mountain opener" in the culture of exorcism prevailed in Pingxiang. They helped us visualize the folk customs in Shang-Zhou period that people wore exorcist masks to dispel evil and pestilence. This resembles in *Zhou Li* (Zhou Rites), "Fangxiang appeared in red and dark robe. He had four golden eyes, and covered his hands and feet with bare fur. Holding a shield and a dagger-axe in hands, and having hundreds followers under his command, he was ready to fight off demons and pestilence." This folk wizard custom spread from the mid-stream in Yangtze River to the east and the west covering the entire Yangtze River valley, and to the north into Sichuan and southern Shaanxi, connecting with the central plain culture of the middle reaches in the Yellow River. With a history of over 7,000 years since primitive society, the culture of exorcism is like an important live fossil in the study of Chinese historical culture.

If we connect the time and location of all the images and masks, the tiger face with long teeth on the 7,500-year-old pottery from Hunan; the sketches of a tiger with long teeth on the 6,000-year-old ivory ware from Gansu and Shaanxi; and the 5,000-year-old tiger face jade ware with protruding teeth from Liangzhu Culture in Wuxian County in Jiangsu Province; we would see a culture belt of tiger totem stretching all the way from the Yangtze River valley to the Yellow River basin. In addition, we have the bronze masks with ox horns and tiger teeth from the Xin'gan tomb of the Shang Dynasty in Jiangxi, and bronze ox masks from Sanxingdui of the Shang Dynasty in Guanghan, Sichuan; together they formed a very unique image of Chinese "exorcist warrior" to protect the people and their residence in the area.

Through the practice of exorcist ceremonies, dance and theatres, people created a full house of good and vicious characters with different personalities, including father exorcist and mother exor-

Exorcist dance (Pingxiang, Jiangxi).

Exorcist play "Zhang Wenxian" (Guichi, Anhui).

cist in western Hunan and Guizhou; Tang, Ge, Zhou three generals and the high commander in Jiangxi; civil officials and warriors; handsome men and women; fairies and ghost; monks and priests. Following Chinese philosophy and aesthetics, the facial masks were

Wood carving exorcist mask from the Yuan dynasty (profile).

Wood carving exorcist mask from the Yuan dynasty (front).

drawn in a formulized way based on the nature of the characters, and touched up by symbolic colors and decorations. Virtue and evil, beauty and beast, were portrayed most vividly through facial make-ups in figures representing loyal and courageous warriors; upright and virtuous civil officials; handsome young men and beautiful girls; friendly elders; green-faced, long toothed demons and ghosts. Dispelling evil and amplifying the brave and the honest for the peace of mind and a safe and comfortable life are the social base for the very existence of the culture of exorcism through all time.

The unique art style exhibited in the woodcut exorcist masks from the Song, Yuan, Ming and Qing dynasties in the temples of Pingxiang stands out among others in the Yangtze River valley. Carved perfectly straight or rounded, the characters are presented in a simple and natural way, poised, mysterious and ferocious. The woodcut by Chen Tuanfa, a seventh generation of a folk artist family in Pingxiang, is representative of today's art on exorcist masks.

Exorcist masks from the Yuan, Ming and Qing dynasties kept by an exorcist temple in Pingxiang, Jiangxi.

The same unsophisticated style is still largely visible in the art works in the region between Hunan and Jiangxi along the Yangtze River, the very birth place of the culture of exorcism.

The culture of exorcism in its very original mode of evil-dispelling

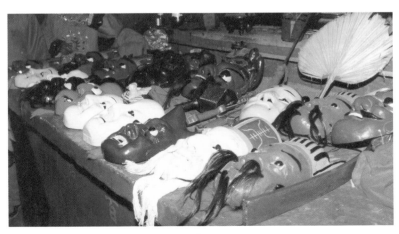

Modern exorcist masks (Pingxiang, Jiangxi).

and fortune-inviting is still well alive among the people in the Yangtze River valley today. It is a live fossil to the study of Chinese ancient historical culture features.

Kite

China is the birthplace of kite in the world, and Henan and Shangdong where people worship birds and the sun were the first to create kite. They still kept the mode of the original kite in Kaifeng today. In my visit to an elder, Mr. Bai Jinsheng, in Kaifeng, he told me that kite was called "Hao" (the sky)

"Swallow kite."

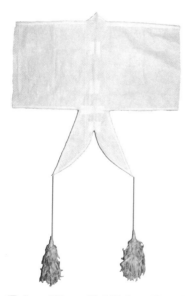

"T-shaped Magua kite" (Kaifeng, Henan).

"Big-feet swallow kite" (Kaifeng, Henan).

"Eight diagrams kite." Photo taken at Nanjing Museum.

in Kaifeng. An old saying goes, "On the third day in the third lunar month, 'Hao' flies up to the sky." It is the time around the Pure Brightness Day when people come out to fly kite by the beach. Guys fly kite and girls play swings. Kite used to be plain white without any painted color or pattern. When the wind is low, flying in the sky is "Magua"

"T-shaped Magua kite" (Taojiang, Hubei).

(Jacket style), and in high wind, it will be "Tong Hao."

The name "Hao" implies the original meaning of kite. Hao means the sky and the sun. The constitution of character "Hao" also shows that the sun is at the highest end of the sky. Therefore, it is believed that flying kite at the time when the land starts warming up can gain access to sun light. Tai Hao and Shao Hao tribes in ancient China were also worshipers of the sky and the sun. The original inhabitants of Shao Hao tribe were around Henan and Shandong, and their tribal emblem was a double-tail swallow, or, in the words of Mr. Bai, the "big feet swallow." Another symbol is the golden crow or a sun bird. Bai referred to it as "one foot swallow" as it has a dovetail. Most of the bird-shaped kites are transformed figures of sun birds or the golden crow. There is also a transformed symbol of a geometry code for perpetual life, referred to by Bai as "Magua," in a "T" shape. "T" is a sky reaching symbol often used for the deceased to imply continued life after death, same as the painting on silk of "T" shaped flag placed on the coffin excavated from the Han Tomb in Mawangdui in Hunan. In Hunan, kites flying in sunny spring days are still a white T-shaped "Magua," a symbol of longevity for the living, and eternity for the dead.

In the course of cultural development throughout history, kite, as an art, has presented a spectacular display in a variety of forms in the blue sky. However, its cultural implication as a symbol of life remains the same at all time.